Faith That Is His

When your
belief is heavy,
His faith is light.

Tracy Huey

Published by Faith That Is His
P.O. Box 447
Belvidere, IL 61008

ISBN 978-1-7337191-0-0

Printed in the United States of America
First Edition First Printing 2019

Scripture is taken from and based on the King James Version of the Bible (KJV).

Strong's Exhaustive Concordance Hebrew and Greek numbers and definitions have been inserted into the text, in some instances, to add clarification. In an effort to more closely match the original text, the author uses: Yahweh (Yah) instead of LORD (all caps). Yeshua instead of Jesus. Messiah instead of Christ. Elohim (El) & Mighty One instead of God. When referring to Yeshua: Master instead of Lord (capital L, small o,r,d).

Note: This book is nonfiction and contains the views and opinions of the author. It is intended to provide helpful and informative material on the subject matter covered. It is produced with the understanding that the publisher and the author are not liable for the misconception or misuse of the information provided.

Dedication

את

This book is dedicated to Mike and Daniel *(Hey bud, Do you know how much I love you?)*, the two most influential men in my life. Thank you for your encouragement, your compassion, and for pushing me forward to finish the work.

It has been an incredible journey thus far, and I pray that in our pilgrimage, we will continue on in the faith that comes from Yeshua, the Faith that is His.

I love you guys!

When the Son of man cometh, shall He find faith on the earth? Luke 18:8

את

Contents

Psalm 1:1-3

1 Blessed is the man that walketh not in the counsel of the unrighteous, nor standeth in the way of sinners, nor sitteth in the seat of the scornful.

2 But his delight is in the law of Yahweh; and in his law doth he meditate day and night.

3 And he shall be like a tree planted by the rivers of water, that bringeth forth his fruit in his season; his leaf also shall not wither; and whatsoever he doeth shall prosper.

Preface

את

Aleph: (THE BEGINNING)
*Looking unto Yeshua the author and finisher of
our faith... (Hebrews 12:2)*

Faith. What is it? In my search to find the
answer to this question, I found no lack of
information available. And in spite of all the
teachings, sermons, books, newsletters, blogs, etc.,
that covered some aspects of this subject, I found
myself continuing to struggle with defining the
indefinable. The question remained, "What is
faith?"

Dear Reader,
Peace and Shalom to all my fellow peculiar
(Deut. 14:2) ones. I pray this book brings you
closer to the One who has called you. And I pray
that in my own inadequate attempts to tear down
walls of deception and build upon the foundation
of truth, that Yahweh would have mercy on me for
my shortcomings.
First, let me apologize to you. Because I have

little experience in writing, nor would I consider myself a writer, you may face some challenges in reading this book. Additionally, you may come across some unfamiliar terms and a different approach to reading, studying and interpreting the Scriptures. But if you are able to hang in there and look past all that, the content contained within this book is solid. I hope and pray you will persist to the end.

So, let me tell you a little bit about myself. I was not raised in the Church and I don't have much of a Church background. As a child, I remember my parents taking us to Church a few times, but never on a regular basis. We also had a family friend who was a Priest and very involved with the family up until I was about six.

Throughout the years, I always had a sense of God *(which was how I referred to Him)* but never had a relationship with Him. It was only after many years of ongoing heartbreak and hardship *(being given up for adoption and losing both parents and grandparents, feeling rejected and alone and all the horrific life decisions and consequences which stemmed from such tragedies)* that I finally turned to Him.

One day back in 2002 *(I would have been 32 at the time)*, I was in my bedroom watching a popular Christian network. Don't ask me why because I didn't regularly watch these shows. When the program host gave a call for the sinner's prayer *(more on that later)*, I prayed along with him. That day changed my life *(in spite of all the times after this I backslid (a Church term), but it is more likely that I wasn't actually saved).* Even though my beliefs have changed significantly since that day, it is proof that Father can use just about anything and anyone to reach those He chooses.

So, this is when my Church life began. Approximately a year later, my husband and I became very involved in a local Church. We were a part of a small congregation and the Pastor was full of patience and mercy. We were young in our walks and zealously foolish, and he put up with all of our childish *(not child-like)* behavior and immaturity. Even though we were heavily involved, we still felt like something was missing *(through no fault of the Pastor)* and kept searching for something that would help fill the void.

This is where things took a turn for the worse. We left that small congregation that had a Pastor with a genuine love for the lost, to a much larger Church, with inspirational teachings, a choir *(at the time)*, and an extremely talented worship team. A perfect Church.

Unfortunately, things went very wrong for us and our lives fell apart. My husband and I went back and forth in our relationship and I kept asking God why? *(which was still the way I referred to Him)* How I see it today, Father was using this time to discipline us because *every father disciplines his children. (Hebrews 12:4-10)* We should have stayed put and continued to grow.

By this time, I felt alone and wandered around

in despair. I left that Church and visited several other Churches, but never quite fit it. Every time I went, there always seemed to be something that just didn't line up with Scripture. And I would ask, "Father, are you here?" I would always try to go back, after all, you are not supposed to *forsake the assembling of the saints (Heb. 10:25)*. But every time I did, I got more and more uncomfortable. It seems Father was leading me into what I now call my wilderness journey.

In these random visits to Churches and in watching Christian Networks, the preachers would teach about faith, but they almost always taught about faith in the same way. I found out later, that much of what they taught about faith was untrue. They equated faith with being able to speak things into existence. As if we were little gods, *(applying Scripture incorrectly)* and calling things that are not as though they were *(again, applying Scripture incorrectly)*. They taught that as believers, we had the power and the authority to receive anything we asked for. But this was contingent upon us believing hard enough, upon us having enough faith. And through their art of manipulating the Word, they were very convincing. I was led astray by my lack of maturity in the Word and by my error of looking to man to teach me instead of looking to the Spirit.

It is only after much stubbornness and hardness of heart, and the tearing down of everything I was standing, praying, and believing for, that Abba Father finally broke through to me and called me out from among them. In His mercy, He helped me to see that this was not faith. Certainly not the faith that is His. And I was embarrassed. After much repenting and tears of thankfulness, I asked Him to reveal to me what it means to have faith. I asked, "Father, what is faith?"

So in 2012 *(ten years later)*, even though I would have considered myself a student of His Word, He opened up the Scriptures and I was seeing things for the first time. By 2015, my excitement caused me to get ahead of myself and I made some attempts at preaching. Even though I learned much from the experience, He made it clear to me that this was not the path He wanted me to take. So, I dusted myself off and continued to seek His will. He then spoke to me about the Sabbath and His Holy Days. By 2017, He told me His name wasn't God *(Yahweh)*. He told me His Son had a name *(Yeshua)* and in His name is Salvation.

As He drew me I sought Him more. The things that the world considered to be important were no longer important to me. I wanted one thing and one thing only, to know Him as He really is. As with Moses I pled, "Show me your glory." He has become so real to me and in His mercy continues to call my name, "Tracy, Tracy?" And my reply is, "Speak, for your servant is listening." He speaks and I listen.

Abba has told me to warn the people *(whether they listen or fail to listen)*, call them to repentance, and point them back to Yahweh. As I follow

Yeshua, I can hear the words of Jeremiah ...*His Word was in mine heart as a burning fire shut up in my bones, and I am weary with forbearing. (Jeremiah 20:9)*

I am so very thankful for everything He has taken me through and kept me through and that He has not let me stray beyond His reach. The journey that I find myself on today, may be a narrow path, but I know He is with me. I look forward to whatever obstacles and challenges that lie ahead because as a child of Elohim, there will be challenges. Yeshua was rejected, persecuted, misunderstood, and judged to the point of being put to death. Not that I would ever face anything in this world that would rise to that level, but whatever I do face, I shall face it with Him and in Him. For what is my life worth if He is not glorified in it?

Why did I write this book?

After Father helped me to discover the true meaning of faith, He told me to share what I learned to encourage others. So, when He told me to put it in a book *(write it down and make it plain Hab. 2:2)*, I was forced way outside of my comfort zone and dared to say, "But Abba Father, I am not a writer." But Yahweh is unrelenting. So, here it is.

Now, I may have made some uncomfortable with my word choice "unrelenting" to describe the Father, but that is the type of relationship we have. It is out of reverent fear that I am able to describe Him in this way, that I am able to describe Him at all. He has been faithful at all times, even when I have been unfaithful to Him. He has taught me about this ever so precious thing called life and has given me unwavering confidence in His love for me. I have come to a point in my walk where I don't need the constant reassurance that He loves me. I see Yeshua and that is all the assurance I need.

The purpose of this book is to encourage those who are still in Church but are heartbroken over the state of the Church or those who have simply left the Church altogether. To those no longer in Church, you may have been told to leave when you asked questions *(which all of us should do)* about what was being taught when it didn't line up with the Scriptures. Or you may have had enough of all the absurdity *(displayed in some Churches)* and have made a choice to come out from among them and be separate *(Isa. 52:11 & 2Cor. 6:17)*.

Many of the mainstream teachings on faith are more about using Yahweh to get what you want out of life. Using Him as if He is a genie in a bottle. Twisting faith as a way of trying to satisfy our own carnal desires. It's more about magic and superstition, then it is about actual faith. And when the magic doesn't "manifest", more often than not, the religious establishment will not take the blame upon themselves for their false teachings but will accuse you of not having enough faith.

Perhaps you feel alone and have cried many

tears. Tears cried on behalf of others and even on behalf of those who mistreated you. But let me assure you that you are not alone and not one teardrop has gone unnoticed by the Father. He sees you. Peculiar one, rejoice! You are among the few.

Why are you downcast, O my soul? Why so disturbed within me? Put your hope in Elohim, for I will yet praise Him, my Savior and my Elohim. (Psalm 42:5)

I pray that the work I have put forth be revealed by fire and may it make it through the flames.

1 Corinthians 3:11-15
11 For other foundation can no man lay than that is laid, which is Yeshua Messiah.
12 Now if any man build upon this foundation gold, silver, precious stones, wood, hay, stubble;
13 Every man's work shall be made manifest: for the day shall declare it, because it shall be revealed by fire; and the fire shall try every man's work of what sort it is.
14 If any man's work abide which he hath built thereupon, he shall receive a reward.
15 If any man's work shall be burned, he shall suffer loss: but he himself shall be saved; yet so as by fire.

The Sinner's Prayer?

Though Elohim, in his mercy will sometimes use the sinner's prayer *(ask "Jesus" into your heart)* to reach people, this practice is nowhere to be found in Scripture. The model for proper evangelism can be found in *Acts 2:22-42*. Peter convicts the people of their wrongdoings *(Acts 2:23 wicked hands)* and accuses them of crucifying the One approved of by Elohim.

Acts 2:36 Therefore let all the house of Israel know assuredly, that Elohim hath made that same Yeshua, whom ye have crucified, both Master and Messiah.

What is their response?

Acts 2:37-40
37 Now when they heard this, they were pricked in their heart, and said unto Peter and to the rest of the apostles, Men and brethren, what shall we do?
38 Then Peter said unto them, Repent, and be baptized every one of you in the name of Yeshua Messiah for the remission of sins, and ye shall receive the gift of the Holy Spirit.
39 For the promise is unto you, and to your children, and to all that are afar off, even as many as Yahweh our Elohim shall call.
40 And with many other words did he testify and exhort, saying, Save yourselves from this untoward generation.

Many times we don't want to come across as being too radical or unloving, so we don't expose man for the evil he has committed. Maybe if I had been convicted of my sin, just maybe it wouldn't have taken me so long to come to the truth and would have spared me a lot of trouble.

As we get closer and closer to the Master's return, the heart of man will grow colder and colder. Men have become so calloused that simply telling them, "You are a sinner and you need a Savior," it not enough anymore. We have to tell them *why they are a sinner* and *why they need a Savior.* Let them accuse you of being unloving. It is not unloving when you tell them the truth. It is unloving not to.

Some focus most of their attention on Yeshua *(Jesus)* and some focus most of their attention on Yahweh *(God).* But this journey requires attention on both. The ultimate goal is to get to the Father, but we can only get to Him through Yeshua. Yeshua points us to the Father and the Father points us to the Son. I imagine Yeshua saying as He stands between us and the Father: "Child, behold thy Father." And to Abba Father, He is saying, "Father, behold thy child."

In Yeshua's Name. Amen.

Introduction

את

The Scripture references in this book are from the King James Bible. The Strong's Exhaustive Concordance is based on this translation and will help you in your own studies.

There are going to be times in this book where you may become frustrated or you may want to skip over the Scripture references, but please hang in there. It is important to first lay a solid foundation, before we start building.

I will be with you throughout this journey. And when you want to give up...remember I will be cheering you on.

Terms Used In This Book

YAHWEH (YHWH) is the name of the Father. Most often seen as LORD (all caps).
Spelled: Yod, Hey, Waw, Hey. Consisting of four letters also known as the Tetragrammaton.

YESHUA is the name of the Son.

MESSIAH means Christ in Greek and Mashiach in Hebrew (Anointed One). Yeshua HaMashiach.

MASTER means Lord (capital L, small o,r,d).

ELOHIM means Mighty One (most often seen as God). Can also mean mighty one(s) or elohim (god(s)) with a small "e".

TORAH refers to Yahweh's Instructions, His Commandments, His Law. Considered the first five books of the Bible.

CHURCH refers to the Institutionalized Church.

EKKLÉSIA refers to what Yeshua said He would build. *(Matthew 16:18)*

MAN refers to mankind (men & women).

Now there are some differences in how the names of the Father and the Son are spelled and pronounced, and there are many different teachings to back up each person's viewpoint. But this book is not about the Names. Among the body of Messiah, there is already enough angst and division when it comes to these subjects. Unfortunately, in an effort to try and convince others to believe in their position, some have unknowingly inflicted pain upon the body, so I will not add to it.

The purpose of this book is to help one learn

the true meaning of faith and how one can find it. There are things I believe Father has revealed to me *(not because I'm special or unique)* and that He has told me to tell others. In my best efforts, I will try to share these things with you. Some of these things may bring about differences of opinion and that's ok. I have learned from past mistakes that it is always better to question than it is to just follow along. My dearest brother, my dearest sister, don't follow any man, but follow Yeshua.

For By Grace Are You Saved Through Faith.

What does that mean? For someone with no religious background, this Scripture is vague and abstract and nearly impossible to define. Even to a believer, this statement is hard to explain. So, here is the challenge. How do we explain this Scripture in a way that is both meaningful and applicable? In a way that will transform the life of an unbeliever as well as a believer.

By the end of this book, you will be able to answer the question, "What is His faith?", and explain "for by grace are you saved through faith." You will be able to describe these in simple concrete terms to just about anybody. I hope you will also learn new and exciting things about Abba Father and His Son. I pray through revelation given to you by the Spirit that you will also be able to use what you learn to make an eternity lasting impact in the lives of those around you.

For Kingdom's Sake.

Psalm 119:105 Thy word is a lamp unto my feet, and a light unto my path.

Chapter 1

את

The Hebrew Alphabet
(Aleph-Bet)

Aleph is the first letter and Taw is the last letter of the Hebrew Alphabet *(Aleph-Bet)*. The Aleph and the Taw, the first and the last. In Greek, it is stated the Alpha and the Omega, the beginning and the end. I begin this book with the Aleph, Yeshua the author, and I end it with the Taw, Yeshua the finisher of our faith. *(Hebrews 12:2)*

The Otiot, which is plural in form, refers to the 22 letters of the Hebrew Alphabet. The Otiot are ancient pictorial *(pictograph)* symbols of each letter. Both Middle and Modern Hebrew letters come from the Ancient Hebrew Alphabet. Ot, which is singular in form, is the Hebrew word for letter, meaning sign.

Ancient Hebrew words are concrete, meaning they can be picked up by our physical senses, while Modern Hebrew, Greek, and Western words

1

are abstract, meaning they come from the mind and are more of a thought or an idea. *(A brief mention: When using the Hebrew Alphabet there is no letter that produces the sound for the letter "J".)*

We have heard the saying, "A picture is worth a thousand words." Because Elohim is infinite, pictographs of the Ancient Hebrew Alphabet can be described using many words. But because mankind is finite, and in hopes to better understand what Yahweh is trying to show us, I will attempt to distill the pictographs down using just a few words.

Genesis 1:6-8
6 And Elohim said, Let there be a firmament in the midst of the waters#4325 mayim: waters, water, *and let it* **divide the waters**#4325 mayim: waters, water **from the waters**#4325 mayim: waters, water.
7 And Elohim made the firmament, and divided the waters#4325 mayim: waters, water *which were under the firmament from the waters*#4325 mayim: waters, water *which were above the firmament: and it was so.*
8 And Elohim called the firmament heaven#8064 shamayim ("im" ending is plural).

#8064 Shamayim: heaven, sky
Spelled: Shin, Mem, Yod, Mem

Shin: pictograph of two front teeth
Cut, divide, devour, consume, destroy.

Mem: pictograph of water
Water, Word, mighty, blood.

Yod: pictograph of an arm and hand
To work, a deed done, a finished work.

Mem: pictograph of water
Water, Word, mighty, blood.

Meaning: Divide (shin) waters (mem) by the work
(yod) of waters (mem).
And: Divide water from water.

Elohim said, *let it divide the waters from the waters (Genesis 1:6).* Using the pictograph, His spoken word actually shows up in the written word for heaven, shamayim. Divide waters by the work of waters. If it wasn't for Yahweh being Yahweh, this would be hard to believe. I use this particular example because it clearly shows how the ancient pictorial symbols of the Hebrew letters can help give an in-depth understanding into the Word of Elohim. I find this remarkable!

As you further your own study:
Hebrew is written and read right to left. Greek is written and read left to right.
Old Testament definitions *(Hebrew)* words come from the Hebrew Concordance.
New Testament definitions *(Greek)* words come from the Greek Concordance.

Proverbs 30:4 Who hath ascended up into heaven, or descended? who hath gathered the wind in his fists? who hath bound the waters in a garment? who hath established all the ends of the earth? what is his name, and what is his son's name, if thou canst tell?

Chapter 2

את

The Hebrew Word for Faith

The first time the Hebrew word for faith is used in the Bible is in *Deuteronomy 32*. Yahweh commands Moses to write down a song and teach it to the Israelites so that it *may be a witness for Yahweh against them. (Deut. 31:19)* In this song, it states that the children of Israel had no faith. The people Yahweh had chosen for Himself out of all the other nations was found without faith.

Deuteronomy 32:20 And he said, I will hide my face from them, I will see what their end shall be: for they are a very forward generation, children in whom is no ***faith****#529 emun*.

#529 Emun: faithfulness; faith (from #539 Aman)
Spelled: Aleph, Mem, Nun

5

Aleph: pictograph of an ox
Father, yoked, strength.

Mem: pictograph of water
Water, Word, mighty, blood.

Nun: pictograph of a sprouting seed
Heir, offspring, descendant.

Meaning: Father (aleph) waters (mem) the seed (nun). And: The strength (aleph) of the blood (mem) is in the seed (nun).

Being that Father waters the seed *(heirs, offspring, and descendants)*, how is it the children of Israel had no faith, when we can look at these events and see faith? We see the Father, we see the water, and we see the children *(seed)*. Why did they lack faith?

Hebrews 3:12-19
12 Take heed, brethren, lest there be in any of you an evil heart of unbelief, in departing from the living Elohim.
13 But exhort one another daily, while it is called Today; lest any of you be hardened through the deceitfulness of sin.
14 For we are made partakers of Messiah, if we hold the beginning of our confidence steadfast unto the end;
15 While it is said, Today if ye will hear his voice, harden not your hearts, as in the provocation.

16 For some, when they had heard, did provoke: howbeit not all that came out of Egypt by Moses.
17 But with whom was he grieved forty years? Was it not with them that had sinned, whose carcases fell in the wilderness?
*18 And to whom sware he that they should not enter into his rest, but to them that **believeth not**#544 apeitheó: to disobey, rebel.*
*19 So we see that they could not enter in because of **unbelief**#570 apistia: unbelief.*

*Hebrews 4:6 Seeing therefore it remaineth that some must enter therein, and they to whom it was first preached entered not in because of **unbelief**#543 apeitheia: disobedience.*

The children of Israel lacked faith because they lacked obedience to Yahweh's instructions. They were rebellious and stiff-necked and chose disobedience over obedience, and the impact of their decisions have had devastating and long-lasting consequences.

Now let us examine the word Emun a little closer. Those that belong to Yahweh are the children of Elohim and they are His seed, heirs, offspring, and descendants. And Yeshua is the Seed.

Father waters the seed and the strength of the blood is in the seed. Yeshua is the Word. And in Yeshua is the strength of the Father. The strength of the Father runs through the blood of Yeshua.

Ezekiel 36:25-29
25 Then will I sprinkle clean water#4325 mayim: waters, water *upon you, and ye shall be clean: from all your filthiness, and from all your idols, will I cleanse you.*
26 A new heart also will I give you, and a new spirit will I put within you: and I will take away the stony heart out of your flesh, and I will give you an heart of flesh.
27 And I will put my spirit within you, and cause you to walk in my statutes, and ye shall keep my judgments, and do them.
28 And ye shall dwell in the land that I gave to your fathers: and ye shall be my people, and I will be your Elohim.
29 I will also **save**#3467 yasha: to deliver *you from all your uncleannesses:*

Yahweh used water in very significant ways. A few examples are, He created the heavens by water, He renewed the earth by water *(the flood)*, Moses was drawn out of water, the Israelites escaped from Pharaoh by passing through water, while in the desert Yahweh provided them water, Yeshua is baptized in water, Yeshua's first miracle involved water *(turns water into wine)*, Yeshua walked on water, water came from Yeshua's side, we are baptized in water, we are born of water, etc.

Father cleanses us with water and takes away our stony hearts. He then gives us a heart of flesh and puts His Spirit within us. He causes us to walk in His statutes and judgments. By and through Yeshua, He saves *(delivers)* us from all our filthiness.

It is so important to recognize that all comes from Him. He is the one that wills it. Thy kingdom come. Thy will be done on earth, as it is in heaven; as it is in the shamayim#8064. For it all originates and it all exists for the one who created it.

Romans 11:36 For from him, and through him, and to him, are all things: to whom be glory for ever. *Amén*#281 *amén: truly (of Hebrew counterpart #543 amen, from #539 aman)*.

His Faith

What is His faith? Yahweh really wanted us to know the answer, because He has one of the Old Testament prophets *(Habakkuk)* quoted several times in the New Testament.

Romans 1:17 ...the just shall live by faith.
Galatians 3:11 ...the just shall live by faith.
Hebrews 10:38 ...the just shall live by faith.

Habakkuk 2:4 ...the just shall live by his faith#530 *emunah*.

In Habakkuk it states: *the just shall live by **His faith***, with the word for faith being emunah. What does this mean? As we look at the spelling of this word using the pictograph, we can see the

9

addition of two letters. The letter Waw *(the nail)* and the letter Hey *(the Spirit)*.

#530 Emunah: firmness, steadfastness, fidelity; *(also comes from #539 Aman)* Spelled: Aleph, Mem, Waw, Nun, Hey

Aleph: pictograph of an ox
Father, yoked, strength.

Mem: pictograph of water
Water, Word, mighty, blood.

Waw: pictograph of a tent peg
Tent peg, nail, firm, secure, join together, becoming bound (nailed to).

Nun: pictograph of a sprouting seed
Heir, offspring, descendant.

Hey: pictograph of a man with arms raised
Behold, to show, reveal, Spirit, worship.

Meaning: Father (aleph) waters (mem) and secures (waw) the seed (nun) with the Spirit (hey). And: The strength (aleph) of the blood (mem) secures (waw) the seed (nun) with the Spirit (hey).

Father waters the seed and secures the seed with the Spirit and the strength of the blood secures the seed with the Spirit. What!!! The strength of the blood of Yeshua secures the children of Elohim with the Spirit! We can now see why the addition of the two letters, the Waw *(the nail)* and the Hey *(the Spirit)*. The Waw represents Yeshua and the Hey represents the Spirit. The just shall live by His faith. The just shall live by His emunah.

Ezekiel 36:26-27
26 A new heart also will I give you, and a new spirit will I put within you: and I will take away the stony heart out of your flesh, and I will give you an heart of flesh.
27 And I will put my spirit within you, and cause you to walk in my statutes, and ye shall keep my judgments, and do them.

Our deliverance and our salvation come by the strength in the blood of Yeshua. The bond that was created by His blood, created by the nail, the Waw; the bond between us and Yeshua, between us and the Spirit, between us and the Father is unbreakable.

John 4:23-24
23 But the hour cometh, and now is, when the true worshippers shall worship the Father in spirit and in truth: for the Father seeketh such to worship him.
24 Elohim is a Spirit: and they that worship him must worship him in spirit and in truth.

This should give us overwhelming confidence.

Not confidence within ourselves, but confidence that comes from the work of Yeshua. His sacrifice was once for all and there is no longer any need for sacrifice. **He is the one that saves!**

Ezekiel 36:29 I will also **save**#3467 *yasha: to deliver you from all your uncleannesses:*

1Peter 3:20-21
20 Which sometime were disobedient, when once the longsuffering of Elohim waited in the days of Noah, while the ark was a-preparing, wherein few, that is, eight souls were **saved by water.**
21 The like figure#499 *antitupos: corresponding to (representing by type or pattern) whereunto even baptism doth also now save us (not the putting away of the filth of the flesh, but the answer of a good conscience toward Elohim,) by the resurrection of Yeshua Messiah:*

Isaiah 12:2-3
2 Behold, **El is my salvation**#3444 *yeshuah; I will trust, and not be afraid: for Yah Yahweh is my strength and my song; he also is become my salvation*#3444 *yeshuah.*
3 Therefore with joy shall ye draw water out of the wells of salvation#3444 *yeshuah.*

El is my Yeshua.
Yahweh is my strength.
Yahweh is become my Yeshua.
Therefore,
Draw water out of the wells of Yeshua.

Emunah: Aleph, Mem, Waw, Nun, Hey

The Aleph. The Waw. The Hey.

The Aleph also represents Yahweh.
The Waw also represents Yeshua.
The Hey also represents the Spirit.

This is *not* the doctrine of the trinity. The trinity is again one of those subjects that has brought much disagreement and division among the body, and I will not add to it.

Deuteronomy 6:4 Hear, O Israel: Yahweh our Elohim, Yahweh is one.

Luke 18:8 When the Son of man cometh, shall
He find faith on the earth?

Chapter 3

את

The Greek Word for Faith

The Greek word for faith *(pistis)* is a Noun. Unlike the Ancient Hebrew Alphabet, which is concrete, meaning it can be picked up by our physical senses, the Greek Alphabet is abstract, meaning it comes from the mind and is a thought or an idea.

#4102 Pistis: Noun *(coming from Elohim)*
Yahweh's divine persuasion, conviction, trust, trustworthiness, assurance, belief, faith, faithfulness

The Greek word for faith *#4102 pistis (used in the New Testament)*, closely matches the Hebrew word for faith, *#530 emunah (used in the Old Testament)*. So, whenever we see *pistis*, we can think *emunah*.

The Greek Word for Believe

The Greek word for believe *(pisteuó)* is a Verb. This word is an action and comes from and originates from self, unlike the Greek word for faith *(pistis)*, a Noun, which comes from and originates from the Almighty.

#4100 Pisteuó: Verb *(coming from self)* to believe, entrust; accept as true, have confidence in, to be persuaded.

When we look at the original Greek words for belief and faith we can see whether the word for belief *(pisteuó)* or the word for faith *(pistis)* is being used in the text. Is it belief *(pisteuó)* coming from oneself, or is it faith *(pistis/emunah)* coming from Yahweh?

Here is a simple way to look at this. Comparing belief and faith is not like comparing apples to apples, but more like comparing apples to oranges. Both are fruit, but they are not the same fruit. *This is not about good fruit vs. bad fruit.* I am just using this as a simple way for us to understand the difference between belief and faith.

Belief says: "I've thought this over and I accept this as truth" *(Comes from self)*.

Faith says: "It doesn't matter what I think, this is truth" *(Comes from Yahweh)*.

Belief is abstract, whereby Faith is concrete.

Faith Came

Galatians 3:23-26
23 But before faith#4102 pistis *came we were kept under the law, shut up unto the faith*#4102 pistis *which should afterwards be revealed.*
24 Wherefore the law was our schoolmaster to bring us unto Messiah that we might be justified by faith#4102 pistis.
25 But after that faith#4102 pistis *is come we are no longer under a schoolmaster.*
26 For we are all children of Elohim by faith#4102 pistis *in Messiah Yeshua.*

Now let's reread this using the Hebrew word for *faith*#530 emunah.

Galatians 3:23-26
23 But before (emunah)#530 *came, we were kept under the law, shut up unto the* (emunah)#530 *which should afterwards be **revealed**.*
24 Wherefore the law was our schoolmaster to bring us unto Messiah that we might be justified by (emunah)#530.
25 But after that (emunah)#530 *is come we are no longer under a schoolmaster.*
26 For we are all children of Elohim by (emunah)#530 *in Messiah Yeshua.*

We can see faith *(emunah)* came in Messiah Yeshua. We are kept under the Law: the Law keeps us *(Gal. 3:23)* until Yeshua is **revealed**. It is

17

the Law that instructs us bringing us to Messiah that we might be justified by Yeshua. After Yeshua, it is no longer the Law that keeps us, but it is Yeshua that keeps us. He keeps us by: *the strength of the blood securing the seed with the Spirit.* For we have become children of Elohim in Messiah Yeshua.

Unfortunately, in Galatians, mainstream teachings have taught on Paul in a manner completely contrary to what he was actually explaining in his letters. In fact, Peter states... *"even as our beloved brother Paul also according to the wisdom given unto him hath written unto you; as also in all his epistles, speaking in them of these things; in which are some things hard to be understood, which they that are unlearned an unstable wrest, as they do also the other scriptures, unto their own destruction." (2Peter 3:15-16)*

Many teach that the Law is done away with. But the Law is Father's wonderful instructions to His children. Without the Law, we are unable to find Yeshua. Father is always pointing us in the direction of His Son, and He uses the Law as a roadmap that will lead us to Yeshua. Father is always saying, *"This is my beloved Son: hear him* (listen to him).*" (Luke 9:35)* In fact, Yeshua is the Law. He is the Torah. He is the Word made flesh. *(John 1:14)*

How can one see themselves as a transgressor, and as such being in need of a Savior, if there is no Law to transgress?

SIN is the Transgression of the Law

What is sin? Instead of looking to man for his own interpretation, let us look at Scripture to see how Yahweh defines sin.

1John 3:4 Whosoever committeth sin transgresseth#458 anomia: lawlessness *also the law: for sin is the transgression*#458 anomia: lawlessness *of the law. (For sin is lawlessness*#458 anomia: lawlessness; without law*)*

Sin is defined as someone who is without Law. They are lawless. Unfortunately, sin is rarely defined correctly in the Church today and the end result is that **sin is left unchecked**. Most, won't even dare to mention sin. In fact, preaching on sin and repentance has been lost. This is one of the main reasons why the Church looks just like the world. We should be telling people the truth, that *sin is lawlessness (John 1:34)* and that *all have sinned (Romans 3:23)* and that *the wages of sin is death (Romans 6:23)*.

Yeshua said...

Matthew 7:21-23
21 Not every one that saith unto me, Master, Master, shall enter the kingdom of heaven; but he that doeth the will of my Father which is in heaven. 22 Many will say to me in that day, Master, Master, have we not prophesied in thy name? and in thy name hast cast out devils? and in thy name done

19

wonderful works?
23 And then will I profess unto them, I never knew
you: depart from me, ye that work iniquity#458 anomia:
lawlessness; without law.

It is unto our own destruction when we reject the Law. No, the Law doesn't save us. **Yeshua is Salvation**. But it is the doing of the Law that shows *(that reveals)* that we are saved.

Yes, be doers of the Law, but keep Yeshua.

2Timothy 4:7 I have fought a good fight, I have
finished my course, I have kept the faith#4102.

Chapter 4

את

The Spirit, the Water and the Blood

We have taken a very close look at the pictographs of the Ancient Hebrew letters for the word faith *(emunah)*. We see the Father, we see the Son, we see the Spirit, we see the water, and we see the blood.

1John 5:5-6
5 Who is he that overcometh the world, but he that believeth#4100 pisteuó: verb (coming from self) to believe, entrust *that Yeshua is the Son of Elohim?*
6 This is he that came by water and blood, even Yeshua Messiah; not by water only, but by water and blood. And it is the Spirit that beareth witness, because the Spirit is truth.

The Spirit testifies that Yeshua came by water and by blood.

1 John 5:7-8
7 For there are three that bear record ~~*in heaven, the Father, the Word, and the Holy Spirit: and these three are one.~~
8 ~~And there are three that bear witness in earth,~~ *the Spirit, and the water and the blood: and the three agree in one.*
    *not found in early manuscripts
1John 5:9-13
9 If we receive the witness#3141 *marturia: testimony, witness, evidence, record of men, the witness*#3141 *marturia: testimony, witness of Elohim is greater: for this is the witness*#3141 *marturia: testimony, witness of Elohim which he hath testified of his Son.*
10 He that believeth#4100 *pisteuó: verb (coming from self) on the Son of Elohim hath the witness*#3141 *marturia: testimony, witness in himself; he that believeth*#4100 *pisteuó: verb (coming from self) not Elohim hath made him a liar, because he believeth*#4100 *pisteuó: verb (coming from self) not the record*#3141 *marturia: testimony, witness that Elohim gave of his Son.*
11 And this is the record#3141 *marturia: testimony, witness,*
Elohim hath given to us eternal life, and this life is in his Son.
12 He that hath the Son hath life; and he that hath not the Son of Elohim hath not life.
13 These things have I written unto you that believe#4100 *pisteuó: verb (coming from self) on the name of the Son of Elohim; that ye may know*#1492 *eidó: be aware, behold, consider, perceive (from the mind; comprehension) that ye have eternal life, and that ye may believe*#4100 *pisteuó: verb (coming from self) on the name of the Son of Elohim.*

The Spirit bears witness that Yeshua came by water and by blood. The one that believes, *(to believe, entrust; and accept as true)* has the witness in himself. And this is the witness *that Elohim has given us eternal life and this life is in Yeshua (1John 5:11).* Like Yeshua, we also come by water and by blood, and *the Spirit beareth witness (1John 5:6).*

By Spirit

By Spirit, we mortify the deeds of the flesh.

Romans 8:13-16
13 For if ye live after the flesh, ye shall die: but if ye through the Spirit do mortify the deeds of the body, ye shall live.
14 For as many as are led by the Spirit of Elohim, they are the sons of Elohim.
15 For ye have not received the spirit of bondage again to fear; but ye have received the Spirit of adoption, whereby we cry, Abba, Father.
16 The Spirit itself beareth witness with our spirit, that we are children of Elohim.

By Water

By water, we are born again.

John 3:3-7
3 Yeshua answered and said unto him, Verily[#281]
amén: truly (of Hebrew counterpart #543 amen: from #539 aman), *verily,*

23

*I say unto thee, Except a man be born again, he
cannot see the kingdom of Elohim.
4 Nicodemus saith unto him, How can a man be
born when he is old? Can he enter the second time
into his mother's womb, and be born?
5 Yeshua answered, Verily, verily, I say unto thee,
Except a man be born of water and of the Spirit, he
cannot enter into the kingdom of Elohim.
6 That which is born of the flesh is flesh; and that
which is born of the Spirit is spirit.
7 Marvel not that I said unto thee, Ye must be born
again.*

By Blood

By blood, we obtain eternal redemption.

*Hebrews 9:11-14
11 But Messiah being come an high priest of good
things to come, by a greater and more perfect
tabernacle, not made with hands, that is to say not
of this building;
12 Neither by the blood of goats and calves, but by
his own blood he entered in once into the holy
place, having obtained eternal redemption for us.
13 For if the blood of bulls and of goats, and the
ashes of an heifer sprinkling the unclean
sanctifieth to the purifying of the flesh:
14 How much more shall the blood of Messiah, who
through the eternal Spirit offered himself without
spot to Elohim purge your conscience from dead
works to serve the living Elohim?*

Where does the Spirit of Elohim reside?

Yeshua's Body

John 2:19-21
19 Yeshua answered and said unto them, Destroy this temple, and in three days I will raise it up. (The three days are explained at the end of this chapter.)
20 Then said the Jews, Forty and six years was this temple in building, and wilt thou rear it up in three days?
21 But he spake of the temple of his body.

The Spirit of Elohim resides in Yeshua.

Our Bodies

1Corinthians 3:16-17
16 Know ye not that ye are the temple of Elohim, and that the Spirit of Elohim dwelleth in you?
17 If any man defile the temple of Elohim, him shall Elohim destroy; for the temple of Elohim is holy, which temple ye are.

The Spirit of Elohim resides in us.

Out of the Belly

John 7:38-39
38 He that believeth on me, as the scripture hath said, out of his belly[#G2836 koilia, #H990 beten] *shall flow*

rivers of living water.
39 (But this spake he of the Spirit, which they that believe on him should receive: for the Holy Spirit was not yet given; because that Yeshua was not yet glorified.)

The Hebrew Word for Belly

#990 Beten: belly, body, womb
Spelled: Beyt, Tet, Nun

Beyt: pictograph of a tent
Tent, house, the body, household, inside, within.

Tet: pictograph of a basket
To surround, to contain, to store.

Nun: pictograph of a sprouting seed
Heir, offspring, descendant.

Meaning: The body (beyt) surrounds (tet) the seed (nun).

Ephesians 1:13-14 ...ye were sealed with that Holy Spirit of promise, 14 Which is the earnest of our inheritance until the redemption of the purchased possession, unto the praise of his glory.

It is our physical bodies that become a place for Him, even though no flesh shall glory in His presence *(1Corinthians 1:29)*. From our physical bodies flow rivers of living waters. The Spirit

26

shall flow from within us. And like Yeshua, we become a temple, the temple of Elohim.

Create a Home for Him

It is a miraculous thing when the Elohim of the universe dwells with man. When He gives His Spirit, His Holy Spirit, to man who is innately evil. And yet, He does not give Himself to just anyone.

Only to those who have built Him a home out of contriteness and humility...

Isaiah 57:15 For thus saith the high and lofty One that inhabiteth eternity, whose name is Holy#6918 qadosh: sacred, holy*; I dwell in the high and holy*#6918 qadosh: sacred, holy *place, with him also that is of a contrite and humble spirit, to revive the spirit of the humble, and to revive the heart of the contrite ones.*

Only to those who have built Him a home out of love and obedience...

John 14:23 Yeshua answered and said unto him, If a man love me, he will keep my words: and my Father will love him and we will come unto him, and make our abode with him.

Only to those who have built Him a home out of salvation, out of Yeshua...

Exodus 15:2 Yahweh is my strength and song, and

he is become my salvation#3444 yeshuah*: he is my El,
and I will prepare him an habitation*#5115 navah: home*;
my father's Elohim, and I will exalt him.*

Those who have prepared themselves as a
home for Him, Yah has become their strength and
salvation and they exalt Him.

Love Yeshua.

John 14:15-21
15 If ye love me, keep my commandments.
*16 And I will pray the Father, and he shall give you
another Comforter, that he may abide with you for
ever;*
*17 Even the Spirit of truth; whom the world cannot
receive, because it seeth him not, neither knoweth
him: but ye know him; for he dwelleth with you,
and shall be in you.*
*18 I will not leave you comfortless: I will come to
you.*
*19 Yet a little while, and the world seeth me no
more; but ye see me: because I live, ye shall live
also.*
*20 At that day ye shall know that I am in my
Father, and ye in me, and I in you.*
*21 He that hath my commandments, and keepeth
them, he it is that loveth me: and he that loveth me
shall be loved of my Father, and I will love him, and
will manifest myself to him.*

The Importance of the Three Days

The scribes and the Pharisees asked Yeshua for a sign:

Matthew 12:38-40 The certain of the scribes and of the Pharisees answered, saying, Master, we would see a sign from thee.
39 But he answered and said unto them, An evil and adulterous generation seeketh after a sign; and there shall no sign be given to it, but the sign of the prophet Jonas:
40 For as Jonas was three days and three nights in the whale's belly; so shall the Son of man be three days and three nights in the heart of the earth.

If Yeshua's words are not perfectly fulfilled, then He is not who He claimed himself to be. And Yahweh forbid that anyone would think such a thing!

Now we can't know for sure if Yeshua was referring to the exact moment He died *(breathed His last)* or if it was the exact moment His body was laid in the tomb. But we can know for sure the time period. Yeshua died around 3pm *(Mat. 27:46)*. And because we don't know the exact time of sunset that day, let's say sunset was around 6pm. To fulfill Yeshua's Words perfectly, He had to be in the grave for three days and three nights (72 hours).

Yeshua died around 3pm on Wednesday. He

29

was placed in the tomb that evening just prior to sunset around 6pm (that evening began a high Sabbath *(John 19:31)*, which can fall on any day of the week *(Mark 15:42)*. If you look at Passover and the Feast of Unleavened Bread you will find that the day after Passover, which is the first day of Unleavened Bread, is always a high Sabbath.

Now the math.
Wednesday 3pm-6pm to Thursday 3pm-6pm = 1 day
Thursday 3pm-6pm to Friday 3pm-6pm = 2 days
Friday 3pm-6pm to Saturday 3pm-6pm = 3 days

Yeshua rose sometime after 3pm and prior to sunset *(6pm)* on the Sabbath (Saturday). Yeshua is Master of the Sabbath *(Mat. 12:8)*. It is important to note that Saturday night at sunset, began their first day of the week (by the time they had gone to the tomb, He wasn't there, He had already risen *(Luke 24:1-6)* and this first day of the week didn't end until Sunday night at sunset.

Now, this is where we can apply belief or faith.

Belief says: "I've thought this over and I accept this as truth" (or not) *(Comes from self)*.

Faith says: "It doesn't matter what I think, this is Truth" *(Comes from Yahweh)*.

Chapter 5

את

Be A Witness

There are those who know nothing of the Law and yet do the Law because the work of the Law is written on their hearts. They are doers of the Law and their *conscience* bears witness.

Romans 2:12-16
12 For as many as have sinned without law shall also perish without law: and as many have sinned in the law shall be judged by the law;
13 (For not the hearers of the law are just before Elohim, but the doers of the law shall be justified.
14 For when the Gentiles, which have not the law, do by nature the things contained in the law, having not the law, are a law unto themselves:
15 Which shew the work of the law written in their hearts, their conscience also bearing witness, and their thoughts the mean while accusing or else excusing one another;)
16 In the day when Elohim shall judge the secrets

of men by Yeshua Messiah according to my gospel.

But what does being a witness have to do with faith? To find the answer, we need to look at the word for conscience.

#4893 Suneidesis: conscience,
A persisting notion;
The soul as distinguishing between what is morally good and bad, prompting to do the former and shun the latter, commending the one, condemning the other; conscience.
(Thayer's Greek Lexicon)

Galatians 5:16-25
16 This I say then, Walk in the Spirit, and ye shall not fulfil the lust of the flesh.
17 For the flesh lusteth against the Spirit, and the Spirit against the flesh: and these are contrary the one to the other: so that ye cannot do the things that ye would.
18 But if ye be led of the Spirit, ye are not under the law.
19 Now the works of the flesh are manifest, which are these; adultery, fornication, uncleanness, lasciviousness,
20 Idolatry, witchcraft, hatred, variance, emulations, wrath, strife, seditions, heresies,
21 Envyings, murders, drunkenness, revellings, and such like: of the which I tell you before, as I have also told you in time past, that they which do such things shall not inherit the kingdom of Elohim.

22 But the fruit of the Spirit is love, joy, peace, longsuffering, gentleness, goodness, faith,
23 Meekness, temperance: against such there is no law.
24 And they that are Messiah's have crucified the flesh with the affections and lusts.
25 If we live in the Spirit, let us also walk in the Spirit.

The Spirit is not given so one may speak in tongues, though one may speak in tongues. The Spirit is not given so one may have the gift of prophecy and fathom all mysteries, though one may have the gift of prophecy. Father gives His Spirit for a very specific purpose and that specific purpose is to serve as a witness for His Son. When we go about seeking a fresh touch of the Spirit, or a new infilling of the Spirit, we should really pause and ask ourselves, "Have I been a witness?" If the answer is no, then why would Father give His Spirit to anyone who will not be a witness for His Son on the earth?

Acts 1:4-8
4 And, being assembled together with them, commanded them that they should not depart from Jerusalem, but wait for the promise of the Father, which, saith he, ye have heard of me.
5 For John truly baptized with water; but ye shall be baptized with the Spirit not many days hence.
6 When they therefore were come together, they asked of him, saying, Master, wilt thou at this time

restore again the kingdom to Israel?
7 And he said unto them, It is not for you to know
the times or the seasons, which the Father hath put
in his own power.
8 But ye shall receive power, after that the Spirit is
come upon you: and ye shall be witnesses unto me
both in Jerusalem, and in all Judea, and in
Samaria, and unto the uttermost part of the earth.

As a witness of Yeshua Messiah, the Spirit will not oppose the Law, the Torah *(Yahweh's instructions)*. Someone who is secured with, filled with, walking in, and being led by the Spirit will not be in the habit of doing things that are in opposition to the Law, such as putting other gods before Yahweh, serving and worshiping idols, taking Yahweh's name in vain, forgetting the Sabbath day, dishonoring parents, murdering, committing adultery, stealing, bearing false witness, coveting, etc. They will not worship the one true Elohim in the way of a foreign god. They are the ones whose character lines up with Yeshua's.

One way to see if our character is lining up with Yeshua's is to examine ourselves to see if we are in the faith *(2Corinthians 13:5)*. Is this something Yeshua would be looking at, listening to, eating, touching, saying, or even thinking? Are we honoring Yahweh with our worship or have we been ensnared by the world causing us to worship the one true Elohim in the way of other gods?

Deuteronomy 12:29-31
29 When Yahweh thy Elohim shall cut off the nations from before thee, whither thou goest to possess them, and thou succeedest them, and dwellest in their land;
30 Take heed to thyself that thou be not snared by following them, after that they be destroyed from before thee; and that thou inquire not after their mighty ones, saying, How did these nations serve their mighty ones? even so will I do likewise.
31 Thou shalt not do so unto Yahweh thy Elohim: for every abomination to Yahweh, which he hateth, have they done unto their mighty ones; for even their sons and their daughters have burnt in the fire to their mighty ones.

Now to answer the question, what does being a witness have to do with faith? Those who say they have faith must be a witness of Yeshua. Those who are a witness of Yeshua must have the Spirit in themselves. Those who have the Spirit in themselves are being *conformed to the image of the Son. (Romans 8:29)* And those who are being conformed to the image of the Son *shew the work of the law written in their hearts, their conscience also bearing witness, and their thoughts the mean while accusing or else excusing one another. (Romans 2:15)*

One can't say they have faith *(the strength of the blood secures the seed with the Spirit)* if they don't walk in the Spirit. If they don't have the witness. *For the flesh lusteth against the Spirit and*

35

the Spirit against the flesh. (Gal. 5:17) If one says they have the Spirit and yet walk after the flesh, they are hypocrites. And Yeshua has a very strict warning for those who say one thing and yet do another. *(Matthew 23:13-33 Woe unto you, scribes and Pharisees, you hypocrites*#5273 *hupokrités: one who answers, an actor, a hypocrite; pretender ...ye serpents, ye generation of vipers, how can ye escape the damnation of hell?)*

If we say we have faith then we must be a witness by having the witness.

Hypocrisy

Hypocrisy can be defined as someone who says one thing and does another, but it can also be defined as someone who does one thing and lacks doing the other.

Matthew 23:14 Woe unto you, scribes and Pharisees, hypocrites! for ye devour widows' houses, and for a pretence make long prayer: therefore ye shall receive the greater damnation.

Matthew 23:23 Woe unto you, scribes and Pharisees, hypocrites! for ye pay tithe of mint and anise and cummin, and have omitted the weightier matters of the law, judgment, mercy, and faith: these ought ye to have done, and not to leave the other undone.

We know for certain that the scribes and Pharisees were *doers of the law (Romans 2:13)*. But Yeshua said they were hypocrites. They said one thing and did another. They said long-winded prayers and yet devoured widows' houses. They also did one thing and lacked doing the other. They tithed but omitted judgment, mercy, and faith.

We can see from their hypocrisy that they lacked having the Spirit. In fact, they lacked having the Spirit *(the witness of Yeshua)* so much so, that when Messiah appeared, they missed Him. They missed the Messiah! They missed the One they had been waiting for all their lives. The religious leaders who studied Torah, who lived Torah, who studied the Prophets, and knew everything there was to know about the Messiah, and they were earnestly looking for Him, didn't recognize Him when He showed up.

How tragic. They were so busy searching the Scriptures *(John 5:39)* and being doers of the Law, that when the Word made flesh appeared, they were unable to see Him for who He was. The Son of Elohim. They were incapable of seeing the truth. What caused such blindness? Pride. They knew the Law, so there was no way anyone, not even Yeshua could convince them otherwise.

John 7:45-49
45 Then came the officers to the chief priest and Pharisees; and they said unto them, Why have ye not brought him?

46 The officers answered, Never man spake like this man.
47 Then answered them the Pharisees, Are ye also deceived?
48 Have any of the rulers or of the Pharisees believed on him?
49 But this people who knoweth not the law are cursed.

They were blinded by pride. And their pride also led them to add to the Word of Elohim.

Deuteronomy 4:2 Ye shall not add unto the word which I command you, neither shall ye diminish aught from it, that ye may keep the commandments of Yahweh your Elohim which I command you.

Adding to the Word of Elohim, placed heavy burdens upon the converts.

Matthew 23:1-13
1 Then spake Yeshua to the multitude, and to his disciples,
2 Saying, The scribes and the Pharisees sit in Moses' seat:
3 All therefore whatsoever they bid you observe, that observe and do; but do not ye after their works: for they say, and do not.
4 For they bind heavy burdens and grievous to be borne, and lay them on men's shoulders; but they themselves will not move them with one of their fingers.

5 But all their works they do for to be seen of men: they make broad their phylacteries, and enlarge the borders of their garments,
6 And love the uppermost rooms at feasts, and the chief seats in the synagogues,
7 And greetings in the markets, and to be called of men, Rabbi, Rabbi.
8 But be not ye called Rabbi: for one is your Master, even Messiah; and all ye are brethren.
9 And call no man your father upon the earth: for one is your Father, which is in heaven.
10 Neither be ye called masters: for one is your Master, even Messiah.
11 But he that is greatest among you shall be your servant.
12 And whosoever shall exalt himself shall be abased; and he that shall humble himself shall be exalted.
13 But woe unto you, scribes and Pharisees, hypocrites!

May we listen to Yeshua's warning and apply it to our own lives, for whatever it is that we think we know, we don't yet know.

1Corinthians 8:2 And if any man think that he knoweth anything, he knoweth nothing yet as he ought to know.

And whatever it is that we know, it is not our own doing, but His.

1Corinthians 4:7 For who maketh thee to differ from another? and what hast thou that thou didst not receive? now if thou didst receive it, why dost thou glory, as if thou hadst not received it?

And to emphasize further, even with all that we know, we only know in part.

1Corinthians 13:9-12
9 For we know in part, and we prophesy in part.
10 But when that which is perfect is come, then that which is in part shall be done away.
11 When I was a child, I spake as a child, I understood as a child, I thought as a child: but when I became a man, I put away childish things.
12 For now we see through a glass, darkly; but then face to face: now I know in part; but then shall I know even as also I am known.

Chapter 6

את

Pride vs. Faith

Pride is often accepted and even encouraged. Man in his sinful state is always looking for reasons to be proud. The flesh loves to look for fault in others because when it can make someone else appear inferior, it feels superior and it boasts. The flesh, which is really self, loves to boast. We want to be proud of our talents and abilities, our accomplishments, our race, our gender, our nationality, our favorite sports team, and all the things mankind loves to boast about. But what does Yahweh think about pride?

Proverbs 16:5 Every one that is proud# 1362 gabah: high, proud *in heart is an abomination*#8441 toebah: abomination (loathsome, detestable) *to Yahweh: though hand join in hand, he shall not be unpunished.*

How is it that we never view pride as an abomination? It appears satan has been mighty

41

clever when it comes to pride. He has been able to trick man into *falling for pride* and into *falling because of pride*. It is one of his greatest schemes.

1John 2:16 For all that is in the world, the lust of the flesh, and the lust of the eyes, and the pride of life, is not of the Father, but is of the world.

The devil Used Pride to Tempt Man.

Genesis 3:1-6
1 Now the serpent was more subtle than any beast of the field which Yahweh Elohim had made. And he said unto the woman, Yea, hath Elohim said, Ye shall not eat of every tree of the garden?
2 And the woman said unto the serpent, We may eat of the fruit of the trees of the garden:
3 But of the fruit of the tree which is in the midst of the garden, Elohim hath said, Ye shall not eat of it, neither shall ye touch it, lest ye die.
4 And the serpent said unto the woman, Ye shall not surely die:
5 For Elohim doth know that in the day ye eat thereof, then your eyes shall be opened, and ye shall be as mighty ones, knowing good and evil.
6 And when the woman saw that the tree was good for food (**lust of the flesh**), *and that it was pleasant to the eyes* (**lust of the eyes**), *and a tree to be desired to make one wise* (**pride of life**), *she took of the fruit thereof, and did eat, and gave also unto her husband with her; and he did eat.*

The devil Used Pride to Tempt Yeshua.

Luke 4:3-13
3 And the devil said unto him, If thou be the Son of Elohim, command this stone that it be made bread (**lust of the flesh**).
4 And Yeshua answered him, saying, It is written, That man shall not live by bread alone, but by every word of Elohim.
5 And the devil, taking him up into an high mountain, showed unto him all the kingdoms of the world (**lust of the eyes**) *in a moment of time.*
6 And the devil said unto him, All this power will I give thee, and the glory of them: for that is delivered unto me; and to whosoever I will I give it.
7 If thou therefore wilt worship me, all shall be thine.
8 And Yeshua answered and said unto him, Get thee behind me, Satan: for it is written, Thou shalt worship Yahweh thy Elohim, and him only shalt thou serve.
9 And he brought him to Jerusalem, and set him on a pinnacle of the temple (**pride of life**), *and said unto him, If thou be the Son of Elohim, cast thyself down from hence:*
10 For it is written, He shall give his angels charge over thee, to keep thee:
11 And in their hands they shall bear thee up, lest at any time thou dash thy foot against a stone.
*12 And Yeshua answering said unto him, It is said, Thou **shalt not tempt** Yahweh thy Elohim.*
13 And when the devil had ended all the

43

temptation, he departed from him for a season.

Warning! Pride equates to tempting Yahweh. When we possess pride, we are lacking faith. Faith and pride do not mix. Pride says I am in control of my own life. Pride puffs up and causes one to say, I have power, I have authority, I bind this and I loose that, and I speak this and I command that *(and other dangerous comments one will hear spoken).* We need to be very careful *(Acts 19:15 And the evil spirit answered and said, Yeshua I know, and Paul I know; but who are ye?),* because any power and any authority we may have only comes to us through Yeshua. It's not actually our power or authority, **it's His!**

Instead of behaving as brute beasts and being the cause of our own destruction *(2Pet. 2:12 & Jude 1:10),* let us use caution and seek His guidance and let Yahweh do the rebuking.

An Evil Conscience

Earlier, we defined conscience as:

The soul as distinguishing between what is morally good and bad, prompting to do the former and shun the latter, commending the one, condemning the other; conscience.

But what does it mean to have an evil conscience?

Hebrews 10:19-22
19 Having therefore, brethren, boldness to enter into the holiest by the blood of Yeshua,
20 By a new and living way, which he hath consecrated for us, through the veil, that is to say his flesh;
21 And having an high priest over the house of Elohim;
22 Let us draw near with a true heart in full assurance of faith having our hearts sprinkled from an evil conscience, and our bodies washed with pure water...

We know that all mankind has a conscience. Having a conscience means the ability to know right from wrong and *choosing to do the right* and not to do the wrong.

Therefore, an evil conscience means the ability to know right from wrong and *choosing to do the wrong* and not to do the right. This person chooses to do evil over good.

Hebrews 10:23-29
23 Let us hold fast the profession of our faith#1680 elpis: **expectation, hope** *without waving; (for he is faithful*#4103 pistos: faithful, reliable *that promised;)*
24 And let us consider one another to provoke unto love and to good works:
25 Not forsaking the assembling of ourselves together, as the manner of some is; but exhorting one another: and so much the more, as you see the day approaching.

*26 For if we sin willfully (**evil conscience: choosing to do wrong over right**) after that we have received the knowledge of the truth, there remaineth no more sacrifice for sins,*
27 But a certain fearful looking for of judgment and fiery indignation, which shall devour the adversaries.
28 He that despised Moses' law died without mercy under two or three witnesses:
29 Of how much more sorer punishment, suppose ye shall he be thought worthy who hath trodden under foot the Son of Elohim, and hath counted the blood of the covenant, wherewith he was sanctified an unholy thing, and hath insulted the Spirit of grace?

When we sin willfully, where is faith? Have we trampled on Yeshua? Have we treated the blood of the covenant as unholy? Have we insulted the Spirit who bears witness of Yeshua? Have we had our consciences seared as with a hot iron?

1 Timothy 4:1-2
1 Now the Spirit speaketh expressly, that in the latter times some shall depart from the faith[#4102], giving heed to seducing spirits, and doctrines of devils;
2 Speaking lies in hypocrisy; having their conscience seared with a hot iron;

I believe that when someone departs from the faith, the Father grieves. A person who knows right from wrong, but chooses to do the wrong anyway, that person has a conscience that is evil. As we look around at society today, we are able to see this in action. Many have become accustomed to what the world sees and accepts as right and wrong.

The standard has become man's and not Yeshua's.

Man goes about comparing himself to other men when he should be comparing himself to the only One that matters. To Yeshua. In his sin, man wants to wrap himself up in what he thinks is *grace* and run to the throne. But if man could grasp the magnitude and enormity of his sin, he would not run, but crawl. He would fall on his face and pray, "Abba Father, have mercy on me, a sinner."

We should be diligently seeking Yahweh and asking Him to show us what He sees and accepts as righteous and unrighteous, good and evil, right and wrong. Unfortunately, many have succumbed to the world's standards and as such have consciously departed from the faith.

Ezekiel 33:11 Say unto them, As I live, saith Yahweh Elohim, I have no pleasure in the death of the wicked; but that the wicked turn from his way and live: turn ye, turn ye from your evil ways; for why will ye die, O house of Israel?

Chapter 7

את

Faith Is

Faith is not an abstract thought confined within the barriers of our minds. And faith is not positive thinking.

Hebrews 11:1 Now faith[#4102 pistis] *is the substance of things hoped for the evidence of things not seen.*

As we attempt to define this piece of Scripture, remember the Greek word for faith is *#4102 pistis* and equates to the Hebrew word for faith *#530 emunah*. And also remember *#4102 pistis* is a Noun and always comes from Elohim. *(Yahweh's divine persuasion)*

Hebrews 11:1 Now faith[#4102 pistis (#530 emunah)] *is the substance of things hoped for the evidence of things not seen.*

Faith is the Substance

Hebrews 11:1 Now faith#4102 *(#530 emunah) is the substance*#5287 hupostasis *of things hoped for...*

The Greek Word for Substance

#5287 Hupostasis: a support, substance, steadiness, hence assurance

Yeshua is the substance *(support).* Emunah is spelled Aleph, Mem, **Waw**, Nun, Hey. Remember the WAW *(the nail)* also represents Yeshua. He is the center, the middle, the anchor, the foundation, the support.

Hebrews 6:19-20
19 Which hope we have as an **anchor** *of the soul, both sure and steadfast, and which entereth into that within the veil.*
20 Whither the forerunner is for us entered, even Yeshua, made an high priest for ever after the order of Melchisedec.

Hebrews 11:1 Now faith#4102 *(#530 emunah) is the* (anchor, support, steadiness, assurance)#5287 *of things hoped for...*

Faith is the Evidence

Hebrews 11:1 Now faith#4102 *(#530 emunah) is...the evidence*#1650 *of things not seen.*

The Greek Word for Evidence

#1650 Elegchos: a proof, test, reproof

Hebrews 11:1 Now faith#4102 *(#530 emunah) is... the* (proof, test; reproof, conviction)#1650 *of things not seen.*

The Spirit is the evidence *(proof)*. Remember the Hey *(behold, to show, reveal)* also represents the Spirit.

John 16:7-15
7 Nevertheless I tell you the truth; It is expedient for you that I go away: for if I go not away, the Comforter will not come unto you; but if I depart, I will send him unto you.
8 And when he is come, he will reprove the world of sin, and of righteousness, and of judgment:
9 Of sin, because they believe not on me;
10 Of righteousness, because I go to my Father, and ye see me no more;
11 Of judgment, because the prince of this world is judged.
12 I have yet many things to say unto you, but ye cannot bear them now.
13 Howbeit when he, the Spirit of truth, is come, he will guide you into all truth: for he shall not speak of himself; but whatsoever he shall hear, that shall he speak: and he will shew you things to come.
14 He shall glorify me: for he shall receive of mine, and shall show it unto you.

15 All things that the Father hath are mine: therefore said I, that he shall take of mine, and shall show it unto you.

EMUNAH: Aleph, Mem, Waw, Nun, Hey

Hebrews 11:1 Now faith#4102 *(#530 emunah)* *is the substance* (Yeshua) *of things hoped for, the evidence* (Spirit) *of things not seen.*

Faith is not some penetrable object we are unable to take hold of. No. Faith is tangible. Faith has weight, density, and mass. Faith is the substance of Yeshua. But in order for one to experience Him in this way, one must have the evidence of the Spirit. Otherwise, it is foolishness to them.

1Corinthians 2:9-16
9 But as it is written, Eye hath not seen, nor ear heard, neither entered into the heart of man, the things which Elohim hath prepared for them that love him.
10 But Elohim hath revealed them unto us by his Spirit: for the Spirit searcheth all things, yea, the deep things of Elohim.
11 For what man knoweth the things of a man, save the spirit of man which is in him? even so the things of Elohim knoweth no man, but the Spirit of Elohim.
12 Now we have received, not the spirit of the world, but the spirit which is of Elohim; that we might know the things that are freely given to us of Elohim.

13 Which things also we speak, not in the words which man's wisdom teacheth, but which the Spirit teacheth; comparing spiritual things with spiritual.
14 But the natural man receiveth not the things of the Spirit of Elohim: for they are foolishness unto him: neither can he know them, because they are spiritually discerned.
15 But he that is spiritual judgeth all things, yet he himself is judged of no man.
16 For who hath known the mind of the Master, that he may instruct him? But we have the mind of Messiah.

Faith. Abba Father's divine persuasion made manifest in Yeshua and revealed by the Spirit.

John 3:8 The wind bloweth where it listeth, and thou hearest the sound thereof, but canst not tell whence it cometh, and whither it goeth: so is every one that is born of the Spirit.

Chapter 8

את

Faith & Works vs.
Belief & Works

Faith & Works.
Work that is produced because of our faith.
Works done by faith.

Belief & Works.
Work that is produced because of our belief.
Works done by belief.

Romans 14:23 ...for whatsoever is not of faith[#4102] *is sin.* (Wow, that's a hard word.)

In Romans Chapter 14, Paul is addressing a problem some of the believers were having between belief and faith. *Him that is weak in the faith receive ye, but not to doubtful disputations. (Romans 14:1)*

When read in context, we can see that some

were abstaining from meat, *For one believeth*#4100 *that he may eat all things: another, who is weak, eateth herbs (vs. 2),* and we can see that some were probably fasting on certain days, *Let not him that eateth despise him that eateth not (vs 3.)*

When we read Romans 14, our Western mindset will automatically default to the belief that Paul is saying we can eat all things. A man *of the stock of Israel, of the tribe of Benjamin, an Hebrew of the Hebrews (Philippians 3:5),* was not talking about eating pig, etc. This isn't about clean and unclean. The fact is that all food is clean, if it is actually food, as defined by Yahweh in Leviticus Chapter 11. There is no such thing as unclean food.

Now that I've digressed, let us get back to what Paul was actually saying. He was pointing out that some believed in what they were doing *(the works done by belief),* but at the same time they also doubted *(unbelief).*

Romans 14:23 And he that doubteth is damned if he eat, because he eateth not of faith: for whatsoever is not of faith is sin.

We know that demons believe *(James 2:19).* Think this over for a minute. Where do you think the works of the devil come from? *...For this purpose the Son of Elohim was manifested, that he might destroy the works of the devil. (1John 3:8)* The works come from their belief. They believe in Elohim and this belief even makes them tremble.

And yet, they continue to work. They are constantly at work trying to undo the work of Elohim. They are trying to undo the work that comes from faith. This is the ongoing battle between faith & works vs. belief & works.

Whatsoever is not of faith is sin and sin is the transgression of the Law. If our works are not coming from the Father and being done through Yeshua and going back to Him by the Spirit...

Romans 11:36 For of Him, and through Him, and to Him, are all things: to whom be glory for ever. Amen.

Then our works are being done in the flesh. Works coming from the flesh are not of faith...

Galatians 6:7-8 Be not deceived; Elohim is not mocked: for whatsoever a man soweth, that shall he also reap. 8 For he that soweth to his flesh shall of the flesh reap corruption; but he that soweth to the Spirit shall of the Spirit reap life everlasting.

And work that is not of faith is sin...

Romans 14:23 ...for whatsoever is not of faith is sin.

And sin is the transgression of the Law...
1John 3:4 ...for sin is the transgression of the law.

Belief is important, but *faith* is essential.

57

Unfortunately, most of what we do today stems from belief. But in order for us to impact this world for eternity, we must *do works that stem from faith.* We have been created to do so.

Ephesians 2:10 For we are his workmanship, created in Messiah Yeshua unto good works, which Elohim hath before ordained that we should walk in them.

Chapter 9

את

His Word Remains

In *Matthew 24:35*, Yeshua said that in the last days, *"Heaven and earth shall pass away, but my words shall not pass away."* His words will never pass away. Faith enables us to hang on His every word. The Spirit will not oppose Yeshua, who is the Word. The Spirit will not oppose the Law, the Torah *(Yahweh's instructions)*. If we are filled with, being led by and secured with His Spirit, then we will keep His instructions. We will keep His word, by virtue of the Spirit.

Romans 3:20-31
20 Therefore by the deeds of the law there shall no flesh be justified in his sight: for by the law is the knowledge of sin.
21 But now the righteousness of Elohim without the law is manifested, being witnessed by the law and the prophets;
22 Even the righteousness of Elohim which is by

faith#4102 *of Yeshua Messiah unto all and upon all them that believe: for there is no difference:*
23 For all have sinned, and come short of the glory of Elohim;
24 Being justified freely by his grace#5485 charis: grace, kindness *through the redemption that is in Messiah Yeshua:*
25 Whom Elohim hath set forth to be a propitiation through faith#4102 *in his blood, to declare his righteousness for the remission of sins that are past, through the forbearance of Elohim;*
26 To declare, I say, at this time his righteousness: that he might be just, and the justifier of him which believeth in Yeshua.
27 Where is boasting then? It is excluded. By what law? of works? Nay: but by the law of faith#4102.
28 Therefore we conclude that a man is justified by faith#4102 *without the deeds of the law.*
29 Is he the Elohim of the Jews only? is he not also of the Gentiles? Yes, of the Gentiles also:
30 Seeing it is one Elohim, which shall justify the circumcision by faith#4102, *and uncircumcision through faith*#4102.
31 Do we then make void the law through faith#4102? *Elohim forbid: yea, we establish the law.*

Because His Word remains, it is through faith that we establish the Law *(which is His word).* We are establishing the Law not by works even though we are doing the works, but the works we do are through faith. The works are the evidence of our faith. We are combining faith with works and through faith we establish the Law.

Hebrews 4:2 For unto us was the gospel preached, as well as unto them: but the word preached did not profit them, not being mixed with faith#4102 in them that heard it.

We are justified by faith, without the works of the Law, but without the works, our faith is futile.

James 2:17-24
17 Even so faith#4102, if it hath not works, is dead, being alone.
18 Yea, a man may say, Thou hast faith#4102, and I have works: show me thy faith#4102 without thy works, and I will show thee my faith#4102 by my works.
19 Thou believest#4100 pisteuó that there is one Elohim; thou doest well: the devils also believe#4100 pisteuó and tremble.
20 But wilt thou know, O vain man, that faith#4102 without works is dead?
21 Was not Abraham our father justified by works, when he had offered Isaac his son upon the altar?
22 Seest thou how faith#4102 wrought with his works, and by works was faith#4102 made perfect?
23 And the scripture was fulfilled which saith, Abraham believed Elohim, and it was imputed unto him for righteousness: and he was called the friend of Elohim.
24 Ye see then how that by works a man is justified, and not by faith#4102 only.

Nobody is saved by doing the works of the Law, it is doing the works of the Law that shows we are saved. If we say we know Him, we will walk as He did.

1John 2:3-6
3 And hereby we do know that we know him, if we keep his commandments.
4 He that saith, I know him, and keepeth not his commandments, is a liar, and the truth is not in him.
5 But whoso keepeth his word, in him verily is the love of Elohim perfected: hereby know we that we are in him.
6 He that saith he abideth in him ought himself also so to walk, even as he walked.

Why so much focus on the Law?

Because it blesses us.

Psalm 1:1-2
1 Blessed is the man that walketh not in the counsel of the wicked, nor standeth in the way of sinners, nor sitteth in the seat of the scornful.
2 But his delight is in the law#8451 torah of Yahweh; and in his law#8451 torah doth he meditate day and night.
Because it instructs us.

Psalm 119:33-40
33 Teach me, O Yahweh, the way of thy statutes;

and I shall keep it unto the end.

34 Give me understanding, and I shall keep thy law#8451 *torah; yea, I shall observe it with my whole heart.*

35 Make me to go in the path of thy commandments; for therein do I delight.

36 Incline my heart unto thy testimonies, and not to covetousness.

37 Turn away mine eyes from beholding vanity; and quicken thou me in thy way.

38 Stablish thy word unto thy servant, who is devoted to thy fear.

39 Turn away my reproach which I fear: for thy judgments are good.

40 Behold, I have longed after thy precepts: quicken me in thy righteousness.

Because it frees us.

Psalm 119:44-45

44 So shall I keep thy law continually for ever and ever.

45 And I will walk at liberty#7342 *rachab: wide, broad: for I seek thy precepts.*

And it Shows That Yahweh is Our Elohim.

Deuteronomy 26:16-18

16 This day Yahweh thy Elohim hath commanded thee to do these statutes and judgments: thou shalt therefore keep and do them with all thine heart, and with all thy soul.

*17 Thou hast avouched (declared) Yahweh this day to be thy Elohim, and to walk in his ways, and to keep his statutes, and his commandments, and his judgments, and to hearken unto his voice:
18 And Yahweh hath avouched (declared) thee this day to be his peculiar people, as he hath promised thee, and that thou shouldest keep all his commandments;*

The word for liberty in *Psalm 119:45* means wide or broad *(wide open spaces)*. Let's imagine a caged bird for a moment. The bird will attempt to fly around in the cage, but it is only after the cage door opens that the bird is able to fly free. The world will try to convince us that the Law is the cage. When in fact, lawlessness is the cage. So, without the Law, we are like that caged bird. We are trapped and confined. We have been prevented from being and from doing what Father has created us to be and to do. If we want to be set free from the cage, we must have the key. The Law is the key. When we embrace, the Law, the cage door opens and we are set free. We fly out of the cage into wide open spaces, because in the Law is freedom.

Chapter 10

את

Has the Law Been Done Away With?

We need to look to Yeshua to find the answer to this question.

Matthew 5:17-18
17 Think not that I am come to destroy#2647 *kataluó to destroy, overthrow the law, or the prophets: I am not come to destroy*#2647*, but to fulfil*#4137 *pléroó: to make full, to complete.*
18 For verily I say unto you, Till heaven and earth pass, one jot or one tittle shall in no wise pass from the law, till all be fulfilled.

Are heaven and earth still here? Yes. If heaven and earth are still here then the Law remains. Teaching that the Law has been done away with comes from a misunderstanding of what Paul stated in Colossians.

Colossians 2:8 & 2:14-16
8 Beware lest any man#5100 tis: a certain one, someone, anyone *spoil you through philosophy*#5385 philosophia: the love or pursuit of wisdom *and vain deceit, after the tradition*#3862 paradosis: a handing down or over, a tradition *of men*#444 anthrópos: a man, human, mankind, *after the rudiments*#4747 stoicheion: the elements, rudiments, primary and fundamental principles of any art, science, or discipline (religious training) *of the world, and not after Messiah...*
14 Blotting out the handwriting of ordinances#1378 dogma: an opinion, (a public) decree *that was against us, which was contrary to us, and took it out of the way, nailing it to his cross;*
15 And having spoiled principalities#746 arché: beginning (magistrate, power, principality, rule(rs) *and powers*#1849 exousia: power to act, authority, *he made a show of them openly, triumphing over them in it.*
16 Let no man#5100 tis: a certain one, someone, anyone *therefore judge you...*

Paul was talking about the philosophy, the tradition, the basic principles of the world, and the ordinances of men. He was not talking about the Law being nailed to the cross. Therefore, the Law has not been done away with.

Why has Yeshua been misunderstood?

Matthew 5:17 Think not that I am come to destroy#2647 kataluó to destroy, overthrow *the law, or the prophets: I am not come to destroy*#2647, *but to fulfil*#4137 pléroó: to make full, to complete.

66

Man has applied his own interpretation to Yeshua's Words and thinks destroy and fulfill mean the same thing. They hear Him say, *"think not that I am come to destroy the law ...I am not come to destroy, but to destroy."* We can see this is not what Yeshua said. He did not come to destroy, but to fulfill.

Imagine the moon for a moment. On the days when we can see only part of the moon, it doesn't mean that the rest of the moon is not there. We just can't see it. It is the same with the Law prior to Yeshua. When we can see only part of the Law, it doesn't mean that the rest of the Law is not there. We just can't see it. In Yeshua, we can see the entire Law. He reveals it. He fulfills it.

2Corinthians 3:14-16
14 But their minds were blinded: for until this day remaineth the same veil untaken away in the reading of the old testament; which veil is done away in Messiah.
15 But even unto this day, when Moses is read, the veil is upon their heart.
16 Nevertheless when it shall turn to the Master, the veil shall be taken away.

Revelation of the Word comes only through Yeshua by the Spirit. When one does not have Yeshua, even though they may think they have Him, they will misunderstand the Scriptures because the Scriptures are veiled to them. It is only in Yeshua that the veil is taken away.

In the following, it may appear that Yeshua made the commandment harder:

Matthew 5:21-22
21 Ye have heard that it was said by them of old time, Thou shalt not kill; and whosoever shall kill shall be in danger of the judgment:
22 But#1161 de: but, and, now, moreover, indeed now, on top of this *I say unto you, That whosoever is angry with his brother without a cause shall be in danger of the judgment: and whosoever shall say to his brother, Raca, shall be in danger of the council: but whosoever shall say, Thou fool, shall be in danger of hell fire.*

Yeshua did not make the commandment harder, he revealed the intent of the commandment. He did not do away with the commandment that says, *Thou shalt not kill.* He revealed the intent of it by stating, *Thou shalt not kill* (and, now, moreover) *don't be angry with your brother.*

In the following, it may appear that Yeshua added to the commandment:

Matthew 5:27-28
27 Ye have heard that it was said by them of old time, Thou shalt not commit adultery:
28 But#1161 de *I say unto you, That whosoever looketh on a woman to lust after her hath committed adultery with her already in his heart.*

68

Yeshua did not add to the commandment, he fulfilled the purpose of the commandment. He did not do away with the commandment that says, *Thou shalt not commit adultery.* He fulfilled the purpose of it by stating, *Thou shalt not commit adultery* (and, now, moreover) *don't even look upon a woman lustfully in your heart.*

Yeshua & the Ten Commandments
(Exodus 20:3-17 & Deuteronomy 5:7-21)

1. Thou shalt have no other mighty ones before me.
Matthew 22:37-38 Yeshua said unto him, Thou shalt love Yahweh thy Elohim with all thy heart, and with all thy soul, and with all thy mind. 38 This is the first and great commandment.

2. Thou shalt not make unto thee any graven image …thou shalt not bow down thyself to them, nor serve them.
Luke 4:8 …for it is written, Thou shalt worship Yahweh thy Elohim, and him only shalt thou serve.

3. Thou shalt not take the name of Yahweh thy Elohim in vain.
Matthew 5:33-36 Again, ye have heard that it hath been said by them of old time, Thou shalt not forswear thyself, but shalt perform unto Yahweh thine oaths: 34 But I say unto you, Swear not at all; neither by heaven; for it is Yahweh's throne: 35 Nor by the earth; for it is his footstool: neither by

Jerusalem; for it is the city of the great King. 36 Neither shalt thou swear by thy head, because thou canst not make one hair white or black.

4. Remember the Sabbath Day to keep it holy.
Mark 2:27-28 And he said unto them, The sabbath was made for man, and not man for the sabbath: 28 Therefore the Son of man is Master also of the sabbath.

5. Honor thy father and thy mother.
Luke 18:20 Thou knowest the commandments ...Honour thy father and thy mother.

6. Thou shalt not kill.
Matthew 5:21-22 Ye have heard that it was said by them of old time, Thou shalt not kill; and whosoever shall kill shall be in danger of the judgment: 22 But I say unto you, That whosoever is angry with his brother without a cause shall be in danger of the judgment: and whosoever shall say to his brother, Raca, shall be in danger of the council: but whosoever shall say, Thou fool, shall be in danger of hell fire.

7. Thou shalt not commit adultery.
Matthew 5:27-28 Ye have heard that it was said by them of old time, Thou shalt not commit adultery: 28 But I say unto you, That whosoever looketh on a woman to lust after her hath committed adultery with her already in his heart.

8. Thou shalt not steal.
Matthew 19:18 ...Thou shalt not steal...

9. Thou shalt not bear false witness.
Matthew 19:18 ...Thou shalt not bear false witness...

10. Thou shalt not covet.
Mark 7:21-23 For from within, out of the heart of men, proceed evil thoughts, adulteries, fornications, murders, 22 Thefts, covetousness, wickedness, deceit, lasciviousness, an evil eye, blasphemy, pride, foolishness: 23 All these evil things come from within and defile the man.

Be Careful What You Teach

One who teaches the Word of Elohim should be 100% certain that the Almighty is telling them to teach others to reject the Law. Because if they are wrong, they are actually cursing others and damning their own souls.

Ezekiel 3:17-19
17 Son of man, I have made thee a watch-man#6822 tsaphah: to look out or about, spy, keep watch unto the house of Israel: therefore hear the word at my mouth, and give them warning from me.
18 When I say unto the wicked#7563 rasha: wicked, criminal, Thou shalt surely die; and thou gives him not warning, nor speakest to warn the wicked#7563 rasha from his wicked#7563 rasha way, to save his life; the

71

same wicked#7563 rasha man shall die in his iniquity; but his blood will I require at thine hand.
19 Yet if thou warn the wicked#7563 rasha, and he turn not from his wickedness#7562 resha: wickedness, nor from his wicked#7563 rasha way, he shall die in his iniquity; but thou hast delivered thy soul.

Matthew 16:6 & 16:11-12
6 Then Yeshua said unto them, Take heed and beware of the leaven of the Pharisees and of the Sadducees...
11 How is it that ye do not understand that I spake it not to you concerning bread, that ye should beware of the leaven of the Pharisees and of the Sadducees?
12 Then understood they how that he bade them not beware of the leaven of bread, but of the doctrine#1322 didaché: doctrine, teaching of the Pharisees and of the Sadducees.

So, be careful what you teach, because His Words are ever so precious, *Behold, the days come, saith Yahweh Elohim, that I will send a famine in the land, not a famine of bread, nor a thirst for water, but of hearing the words of Yahweh: And they shall wander from sea to sea, and from the north even to the east, they shall run to and fro to seek the word of Yahweh, and shall not find it. (Amos 8:11-12)*
And because His Words are all-consuming, *Wherefore thus saith Yahweh Elohim of hosts, Because ye speak this word, behold, I will make*

my words in thy mouth fire, and this people the wood, and it shall devour them. (Jeremiah 5:14)

Isn't the Law Cursed?

No. No. A thousand times no. It is the breaking of the Law that brings the curse.

Deuteronomy 27:26
Cursed be he that confirmeth#6965 qum: to arise, stand up, stand *not all the words of this law to do them.*

Galatians 3:10
For as many as are of the works of the law are under the curse: for it is written, Cursed is every one that continueth not in all things which are written in the book of the law to do them.

The flesh will always come up with ways to reject the Law. This is why man, who is flesh, uses Paul to try and convince himself that it is ok to disobey. They use a wrong interpretation of what Paul said in Galatians. We first need to understand that Paul was writing to early believers who had previously practiced pagan religions. These early believers faced two obstacles. The strict adherence to Judaism *(the religion)* on one side and former pagan practices *(paganism)* on the other.

Paul had to counter both of these extremes. Judaism, which taught that in order to be saved, one had to keep the whole Law *(Galatians 2:16)* and pagan worship and practices, which included celebrating certain pagan holidays *(Galatians 4:10)*. Both of these were in error. Paul made statements at the time that would later be misinterpreted by some. Paul never believed that the Law was cursed, and as such, neither should we.

Romans 7:12-13
12 Wherefore the law is holy, and the commandment holy, and just, and good.
13 Was then that which is good made death unto me? Elohim forbid. But sin, that it might appear sin, working death in me by that which is good; that sin by the commandment might become exceeding sinful.

The Law vs. Tradition

Tradition is one of the reasons why many believe the way they do. They say, "We've always done it this way" or "It's a family tradition." Tradition itself is not the problem. It is the choosing of tradition over Yahweh's commandments that is the problem.

Matthew 15:2-6 Why do thy disciples transgress the traditions of the elders? for they wash not their hands when they eat bread.
3 But he answered and said unto them, Why do ye also transgress the commandment of Elohim by your tradition?

4 For Elohim commanded, saying, Honour thy father and mother: and, He that curseth father or mother, let him die the death.
5 But ye say, Whosoever shall say to his father or his mother, It is a gift, by whatsoever thou mightiest be profited by me;
6 And honour not his father or his mother, he shall be free. Thus have ye made the commandment of Elohim of none effect by your tradition.

Think about this for a moment. The Law says, honor your father and mother, but tradition says give your money to the Church and then if you have enough, honor your parents. Most Churches *(not all)* teach that no matter what kind of dire straits one might find themselves in, you must give your money *(a certain percentage and then some)* to the Church, and even preach that your finances are cursed if you don't. And some Churches even advocate going into debt by putting it on a credit card.

Unfortunately, for many, after giving their money to the Church, they simply don't have anything left over to honor their parents with. Some can't even afford to take care of their own families. They don't have enough to keep the lights on or food on the table. And in some instances, when someone turns to the Church for financial help, before they say yes or no, they will find out first how much money this person has been giving. How has this become the norm? How is it, when it comes to "tithes" and "firstfruits" *(which always means money),* they tell you to keep the commandments, and yet, when it comes to honoring your parents with the money that they think should go to them, they tell you the Law has been done away with?

Now, I purposely used the word money with giving so as to shine a light in a dark place. The word money has been hidden in the word "give" or "giving". In fact, you will rarely hear them say money at all. Why not call it what it is? When they say give, they really mean give us your money. We should not be opposed to supporting Kingdom work with our money. But we should be opposed to the money making system implemented by the traditions of men. Just something to think about.

Isaiah 3:14
14 Yahweh will enter into judgment with the ancients of his people, and the princes thereof: for ye have eaten up the vineyard; the spoil of the poor is in your houses.

To further clarify tradition... Yeshua said He did not come to destroy the Law *(Matthew 5:17)* and Paul said it is through faith that we establish the Law *(Romans 3:31)*. Not all traditions run in opposition to the Law nor do they run in opposition to faith. But when it comes to tradition, we should ask ourselves, "Why are we doing this?" or "Why do we do it this way?" We better have a good answer because when Yahweh asks, we won't be able to say, "It's a tradition."

Chapter 11

את

All These Blessings Shall Come

We have heard, the Law was or is only for Israel, not the Church. Even though there is one Law for both the native-born and for the stranger.

Exodus 12:49 One law#8451 torah: direction, instruction, law *shall be to him that is home-born*#249 ezrach: a native, *and unto the stranger*#1616 ger: a sojourner *that sojourneth*#1481 guwr: abide *among you.*

Numbers 15:16 One law#8451 torah: direction, instruction, law *and one manner shall be for you, and for the stranger*#1616 ger: a sojourner *that sojourneth*#1481 guwr: abide *with you.*

Many will gladly claim the blessings that come from the Law, all while saying the Law is only for

Israel. You will hear such things as I'm blessed in the city and I'm blessed in the country, I'm blessed going in and I'm blessed going out, I'm the head and not the tail, I lend to many and borrow from none, etc. But what they are missing is the most important thing that does bring the blessings. Keeping His commandments!

Deuteronomy 28:1-14
1 And it shall come to pass, if thou shalt hearken#8085 *shama: to hear (give earnest heed; obey) diligently*#8085 *shama: to hear (give earnest heed; obey) unto the voice of Yahweh thy Elohim, to observe and to do all his commandments which I command thee this day, that Yahweh thy Elohim will set thee on high above all nations of the earth:*
2 And all these blessings#1293 *berakah: a blessing shall come on thee, and overtake thee, if thou shalt hearken*#8085 *shama unto the voice of Yahweh thy Elohim.*
3 Blessed#1288 *barak: to kneel, bless shalt thou be in the city, and blessed shalt thou be in the field.*
4 Blessed shall be the fruit of thy body, and the fruit of thy ground, and the fruit of thy cattle, the increase of thy kine, and the flocks of thy sheep.
5 Blessed shall be thy basket and thy store.
6 Blessed shalt thou be when thou comest in, and blessed shalt thou be when thou goest out.
7 Yahweh shall cause thine enemies that rise up against thee to be smitten before thy face: they shall come out against thee one way, and flee before thee seven ways.

8 Yahweh shall command the blessing upon thee in thy storehouses, and in all that thou settest thine hand unto; and he shall bless thee in the land which Yahweh thy Elohim giveth thee.

9 Yahweh shall establish thee an holy#6918 qadosh: sacred, holy *people unto himself, as he hath sworn unto thee, if thou shalt keep the commandments of Yahweh thy Elohim, and walk in his ways.*

10 And all people of the earth shall see that thou are called by the name of Yahweh; and they shall be afraid of thee.

11 And Yahweh shall make thee plenteous in goods, in the fruit of thy body, and in the fruit of thy cattle, and in the fruit of thy ground, in the land which Yahweh sware unto thy fathers to give thee.

12 Yahweh shall open unto thee his good treasure, the heaven to give the rain unto thy land in his season, and to bless all the work of thine hand: and thou shalt lend unto many nations, and thou shalt not borrow.

13 And Yahweh shall make thee the head, and not the tail; and thou shalt be above only, and thou shalt not be beneath; if that thou hearken#8085 shama *unto the commandments of Yahweh thy Elohim, which I command thee this day, to observe and to do them:*

14 And thou shalt not go aside from any of the words which I command thee this day, to the right hand, or to the left, to go after other mighty ones to serve them.

Reject the Law and Bring On the Curse

There is a level of seriousness to the Law that *(because of Yeshua)*, man has a tendency to overlook. The consequences for breaking the Law brought curses and in some instances even death.

Deuteronomy 28:15-20 & 28:43-46
15 But it shall come to pass, if thou wilt not hearken#8085 shama: to hear (give earnest heed; obey) *unto the voice of Yahweh thy Elohim, to observe to do all his commandments and his statutes which I command thee this day; that all these curses*#7045 qelalah: a curse *shall come upon thee, and overtake thee:*
16 Cursed#779 arar: to curse *shalt thou be in the city, and cursed shalt thou be in the field.*
17 Cursed shall be thy basket and thy store.
18 Cursed shall be the fruit of thy body, and the fruit of thy land, the increase of thy kine, and the flocks of thy sheep.
19 Cursed shalt thou be when thou comest in, and cursed shalt thou be when thou goest out.
20 Yahweh shall send upon thee cursing, vexation, and rebuke, in all that thou settest thine hand unto for to do, until thou be destroyed, and until thou perish quickly; because of the wickedness of thy doings, whereby thou hast forsaken me...
43 The stranger that is within thee shall get up above thee very high; and thou shalt come down very low.
44 He shall lend to thee, and thou shalt not lend to him: he shall be the head, and thou shalt be the tail.

45 Moreover all these curses shall come upon thee, and shall pursue thee, and overtake thee, till thou be destroyed; because thou hearkenedst not unto the voice of Yahweh thy Elohim, to keep his commandments and his statutes which he commanded thee:
46 And they shall be upon thee for a sign and for a wonder, and upon thy seed for ever.

Please don't believe anyone who tells you to reject the Law. Remember there was a time when the children of Israel rejected Yahweh's commandments. They chose disobedience over blessings and this was after they had witnessed all of the miracles that Father did for them. *Deuteronomy 32:20* states *children in whom is no faith.* We can't say we are blessed if we don't obey. And if we don't obey we are just like the children of Israel, *in whom is no faith.*

Shema Israel!

Deuteronomy 6:4-9
4 Hear, #8085 shama: to hear (give earnest heed; obey) *O Israel: Yahweh our Elohim is one El:*
5 And thou shalt love Yahweh thy Elohim with all thine heart, and with all thy soul, and with all thy might.
6 And these words, which I command thee this day, shall be in thine heart:
7 And thou shalt teach them diligently unto thy children, and shalt talk of them when thou sittest

in thine house, and when thou walkest by the way, and when thou liest down, and when thou risest up.

8 And thou shalt bind them for a sign upon thine hand, and they shall be as frontlets between thine eyes.

9 And thou shalt write them upon the posts of thy house, and on thy gates.

Chapter 12

את

What's Going On in the Church?

Unfortunately, with every passing day, the Church is becoming more and more like the world. When I speak of the Church, I am referring to the Institutionalized Church, which looks more like a business then it does like the body of Messiah. Yeshua was perfect, holy, and without sin. Not that anyone through their own efforts can be perfect, holy, and without sin, but if the state of today's Church is evidence, you have to wonder if they even try.

1Peter 1:14-17
14 As obedient children, not fashioning yourselves according to the former lusts in your ignorance:
15 But as he which hath called you is holy, so be ye holy in all manner of conversation#391 *anastrophé: behavior, conduct;*

16 Because it is written, Be ye holy#40 *hagios: sacred, holy (set-apart); for I am holy.*
17 And if ye call on the Father, who without respect of persons judgeth according to every man's work, pass the time of your sojourning here in fear:

The lack of effort to be holy has resulted in the rejecting of his commandments and the committing of all kinds of abominations. The Church looks like the world, lives like the world and yet in their naivety, will still seek His face. What a longsuffering and merciful Elohim He is. The Church needs to heed the warning from the Prophet Jeremiah.

Jeremiah 7:1-15
1 The Word that came to Jeremiah from Yahweh saying,
2 Stand in the gate of Yahweh's house# 1004 *bayith: a house, and proclaim there this word, and say, Hear*#8085 *shama: to hear (give earnest heed; obey) the word of Yahweh, all ye of Judah, that enter in at these gates to worship*# 7812 *shachah: to bow down Yahweh.*
3 Thus saith Yahweh of hosts, the Elohim of Israel, Amend your ways and your doings, and I will cause you to dwell in this place.
4 Trust ye not in lying words, saying, The temple of Yahweh, The temple of Yahweh, The temple of Yahweh, are these.
5 For if ye thoroughly amend your ways and your doings; if ye thoroughly execute judgment between a man and his neighbor;

6 If ye oppress not the stranger, the fatherless, and the widow, and shed not innocent blood in this place, neither walk after other mighty ones to your hurt:
7 Then will I cause you to dwell in this place, in the land that I gave to your fathers, for ever and ever.
8 Behold, ye trust in lying words, that cannot profit.
9 Will ye steal, murder, and commit adultery, and swear falsely, and burn incense unto Baal, and walk after other mighty ones whom ye know not;

(Verse 9 is from The Ten Commandments)

10 And come and stand before me in this house, which is called by my name, and say, We are delivered to do all these abominations#8441 *toebah: abomination?*

11 Is this house, which is called by my name, become a den of robbers in your eyes? Behold, even I have seen it, saith Yahweh.
12 But go ye now unto my place which was in Shiloh, where I set my name at the first, and see what I did to it for the wickedness of my people Israel.
13 And now, because ye have done all these works, saith Yahweh, and I spake unto you, rising up early and speaking, but ye heard not; and I called you, but ye answered not;
14 Therefore will I do unto this house, which is called by my name, wherein ye trust, and unto the place which I gave to you and to your fathers, as I have done to Shiloh.

15 And I will cast you out of my sight, as I have cast out all your brethren, even the whole seed of Ephraim.

When the Church builds, is it really building the house of Elohim? Does it have any resemblance to what Yeshua said He would build? Should we be using the building materials of wood and stone, or the building materials of flesh and blood *(mankind)*? To find these answers let us define Church.

What is Church?

What first comes to mind when you hear the word "Church". Most will think of a Church building or a particular Church or denomination. Usually asked, where do you go to Church? And the normal response is, I go to *(fill in any Church name here)*.

I mentioned earlier my references to Church would refer to the Institutionalized Church. For the most part, this is what we see surrounding us today. Massive and magnificent physical structures designed to amaze the masses *(if you build it they will come)*.

Mark 13:1-2
1 And as he went out of the temple, one of his disciples saith unto him, Master, see what manner of stones and what buildings are here?
2 And Yeshua answering said unto him, Seest thou

these great#3173 *megas: great; large* *buildings? there shall not be left one stone upon another, that shall not be thrown down.*

Yeshua said every stone will crumble. Yes, Yeshua was talking about the temple *(a religious structure)* that would later be destroyed. But it is also likely that He was referring to what will happen in the last days, to *temples made by man (Acts 7:48)* because when you continue on with the rest of *Mark Chapter 13*, you will see Yeshua was describing the end times.

A lot of these Churches like to refer to themselves as the *house of God.* We should not be so quick to think that any physical building is a place the Most High dwells in because He is *Holy! Holy! Holy!* Are these Churches holy? Look what Stephen one of the disciples said, by *the wisdom and the spirit by which he spake (Acts 6:10)* when he addressed the religious establishment.

Acts 7:48-53
48 Howbeit the Most High dwelleth not in temples made with hands; as saith the prophet,
49 Heaven is my throne, and earth is my footstool: what house will ye build me? saith Yahweh: or what is the place of my rest?
50 Hath not my hand made all these things?
51 Ye stiffnecked and uncircumcised in heart and ears, ye do always resist the Holy Spirit: as your fathers did, so do ye.
52 Which of the prophets have not your fathers

persecuted? and they have slain them which showed before of the coming of the Just One; of whom ye have been now the betrayers and murderers:
53 Who have received the law by the disposition of angels, and have not kept it.

This is a strong charge and we should be careful not to follow in their footsteps. Now let's take a look at what Yeshua said He would build.

Matthew 16:18 And I say also unto thee, That thou art Peter, and upon this rock I will build my church#1577 ekklésia; and the gates of hell shall not prevail against it.

Ekklésia#1577: an assembly, a congregation: a calling out, a popular meeting, especially a religious congregation, a community of members on earth or saints in heaven or both, assembly, a people called out from the world and to Elohim.

The Ekklésia is His body.

Colossians 1:24 ...and fill up that which is behind of the afflictions of Messiah in my flesh for his body's sake, which is the church#1577 ekklésia.

The Ekklésia is one body.

1Corinthians 12:12 For as the body is one, and hath many members, and all the members of that one body, being many, are one body: so also is Messiah.

The Ekklésia (being one) is many members.

1Corinthians 12:14-20
14 For the body is not one member, but many.
15 If the foot shall say, Because I am not the hand, I am not of the body; is it therefore not of the body?
16 And if the ear shall say, Because I am not the eye, I am not of the body; is it therefore not of the body?
17 If the whole body were an eye, where were the hearing? If the whole were hearing, where were the smelling?
18 But now hath Elohim set the members every one of them in the body, as it hath pleased him.
19 And if they were all one member, where were the body?
20 But now are they many members, yet but one body.

Being that the Ekklésia is a single body, we are all one in Messiah. If we could understand this mystery *(Ephesians 5:32)*, the world would look radically different then the way it looks today.

An Illustration of the Ekklésia

Ephesians 5:26-32
*26 That he might sanctify and cleanse it with the **washing of water by the word**,* (emunah)

27 That he might present it to himself a glorious church#1577 ekklésia, not having spot, or wrinkle, or any such thing; but that it should be holy and without blemish.
28 So ought men to love their wives as their own bodies. He that loveth his wife loveth himself.
29 For no man ever yet hated his own flesh; but nourisheth and cherisheth it, even as the Master the church#1577 ekklésia:
30 For we are members of his body, of his flesh, and of his bones.
31 For this cause shall a man leave his father and mother, and shall be joined unto his wife, and they two shall be one flesh.
32 But this is a great mystery: but I speak concerning Messiah and the church#1577 ekklésia.

Paul used an illustration of a husband and wife to try and explain the mystery of Messiah and the Ekklésia. Paul was trying to explain the mystery of the oneness of the Father and of the Son and of the Ekklésia.

John 17:20-23
20 Neither pray I for these alone, but for them also which shall believe on me through their word;
21 That they all may be one; as thou, Father, art in me, and I in thee, that they also may be one in us: that the world may believe that thou hast sent me.
22 And the glory which thou gavest me I have given them; that they may be one, even as we are one:
23 I in them, and thou in me, that they may be

made perfect in one; and that the world may know that thou hast sent me, and hast loved them, as thou hast loved me.

The Ekklésia is not a building. It is not somewhere to go *(a location on a map)* and it is not an activity.

It is a people. It is a body. It is His body.

You are the Ekklésia. So wherever you are, there is the Ekklésia.

Revelation 3:21-22 To him that overcometh will I grant to sit with me in my throne, even as I also overcame, and am set down with my Father in his throne. 22 He that hath an ear, let him hear what the Spirit saith unto the Ekklésia.

Chapter 13

את

Understanding Grace

Ephesians 2:8 For by grace#5485 charis: grace, kindness *are ye saved*#4982 sózó: to save; rescue; deliver out of danger and into safety *through faith*#4102*; and that not of yourselves: it is the gift of Elohim:*

To better understand this passage, we need to take a look at the Ancient Hebrew letters for the word grace instead of the Greek letters. The pictograph will give us a concrete meaning of the word versus an abstract thought.

The Hebrew Word for Grace

#2580 Chen: favour, grace, pleasant, precious
Spelled: Chet, Nun

Chet: pictograph of a fence
Protect, separate.

93

Nun: pictograph of a sprouting seed
Heir, offspring, descendant.

Meaning: Protection (chet) of the seed (nun);
Separation (chet) of the seed (nun).
Father protects and separates His children.

Genesis 6:5-8
5 And Elohim saw that the wickedness of man was great in the earth, and that every imagination of the thoughts of his heart was only evil continually.
6 And it repented Yahweh that he had made man on the earth, and it grieved him at his heart.
7 And Yahweh said, I will destroy man whom I have created from the face of the earth; both man, and beast, and the creeping thing, and the fowls of the air; for it repenteth me that I have made them.
8 But Noah found grace#2580 chen: favor, grace *in the eyes of Yahweh.*

During the days of Noah, all flesh had become corrupt on the earth. There was one exception, Noah, who found grace *(chen)* in the eyes of Yahweh. Now when we apply what we have learned about the pictograph of the Ancient Hebrew letters to the word grace, we are able to gain an in-depth understanding of its meaning beyond what is usually taught and defined as unmerited favor.

Why was Noah different from everyone around him? It was because Yahweh had protected Noah and separated him from all other flesh. Yahweh chose a single individual and separated him and protected him from all the others. He did this for Noah, He also did this for the people of Israel and He also does this for us!

Deuteronomy 7:6-9
6 For thou art an holy people unto Yahweh thy Elohim: Yahweh thy Elohim hath chosen thee to be a special people unto himself, above all people that are upon the face of the earth.
7 Yahweh did not set his love upon you, nor choose you, because ye were more in number than any people; for ye were the fewest of all people:
8 But because Yahweh loved you, and because he would keep the oath which he had sworn unto your fathers, hath Yahweh brought you out with a mighty hand, and redeemed you out of the house of bondmen, from the hand of Pharaoh king of Egypt.
9 Know therefore that Yahweh thy Elohim, he is Elohim, the faithful Elohim, which keepeth covenant and mercy with them that love him and keep his commandments to a thousand generations;

Noah, a man of grace, but also a man of faith.

Hebrews 11:7 By faith#4102 Noah, being warned of Elohim of things not seen as yet, moved with fear, prepared an ark to the saving#4991 sótéria: deliverance, salvation of his house; by the which he condemned the world, and became heir of the righteousness which is by faith#4102.

95

It is amazing to see emunah at work in the life of Noah. We see the Father and we see the water and we see the Spirit and we see Yeshua. Noah had faith even before the time of Yeshua. How was that possible?

John 8:56-58
56 Your father Abraham rejoiced to see my day: and he saw it, and was glad.
57 Then said the Jews unto him, Thou art not yet fifty years old, and hast thou seen Abraham?
58 Yeshua said unto them, Verily, verily, I say unto you, Before Abraham was, I am.

John 1:30 This is he of whom I said, After me cometh a man which is preferred before me: for he was before me.

The Meaning

Ephesians 2:8 For by grace[#5485 (#2580 chen)] *are ye saved*[#4982 sózó: to save] *through faith*[#4102]*; and that not of yourselves: it is the gift of Elohim:*

For by *chen* are ye saved through *emunah*; For by *protecting and separating the seed* are ye saved through *the strength of the blood securing the seed with the Spirit.* Father protects and separates us and the blood secures us.

Romans 5:1-2
1 Therefore being justified by faith[#4102]*, we have*

peace with Elohim through our Master Yeshua Messiah:

2 By whom also we have access by faith#4102 into this grace#5485 (#2580 chen) wherein we stand, and rejoice in hope of the glory of Elohim.

The Importance of Grace

It is important for us to see and understand that it is through faith that one gains access to grace. Grace is why we will not be judged by the Law. Righteousness does not come by the Law. Righteousness comes by Yahweh protecting us and separating us through faith in Yeshua. Yeshua is our righteousness. If we could obtain righteousness on our own, through the Law, then Messiah died for nothing.

Galatians 2:21 I do not frustrate the grace#5485 (#2580 chen) of Elohim: for if righteousness come by the law, then Messiah is dead in vain.

Now that Yeshua has come, Yahweh will judge the world by Yeshua. But in order for one to have access to grace, and therefore be judged by Yeshua, one must have faith.

Acts 17:31 Because he hath appointed a day, in the which he will judge the world in righteousness by that man whom he hath ordained; whereof he hath given assurance unto all men, in that he hath raised him from the dead.

Finding Grace in the Wilderness

After Yahweh had miraculously brought the people out of Egypt, and while Moses was on Mount Sinai getting the tablets of the covenant, the people turned away from Elohim.

Exodus 32:1-7
1 And when the people saw that Moses delayed to come down out of the mount, the people gathered themselves together unto Aaron, and said unto him, Up, make us mighty ones, which shall go before us; for as for this Moses, the man that brought us up out of the land of Egypt, we wot not what is become of him.
2 And Aaron said unto them, Break off the golden earrings, which are in the ears of your wives, of your sons, and of your daughters, and bring them unto me.
3 And all the people brake off the golden earrings which were in their ears, and brought them unto Aaron.
4 And he received them at their hand, and fashioned it with a graving tool, after he had made it a molten calf: and they said, These be thy elohim, O Israel, which brought thee up out of the land of Egypt.
5 And when Aaron saw it, he built an altar before it; and Aaron made proclamation, and said, Tomorrow is a feast to Yahweh.
6 And they rose early on the morrow, and offered burnt offerings, and brought peace offerings; and

the people sat down to eat and to drink, and rose up to play.
7 And Yahweh said unto Moses, Go, get thee down; for thy people, which thou broughtest out of the land of Egypt, have corrupted themselves:

We should notice two things right away. One, they were not worshipping a different Elohim, because they said, *"these be thy Elohim"... "which brought thee up out of the land of Egypt."* (Exo. 32:4) So they viewed this idol as Elohim. And two *(now here is something remarkable)*, the idol they created was in the image of a calf. Why a calf? The first letter of the Ancient Hebrew Alphabet is the Aleph, which represents the Father, and it is a pictograph of an ox *(bull, resembles a calf)*.

So again, this reinforces that they were not worshipping another Elohim. And yet they had still sinned against Elohim and broke the commandment by casting Him into an idol. And they knew about the commandment because Yahweh had given it to them back in *Exodus 20*.

Exodus 20:4-6
4 Thou shalt not make unto thee any graven image, or any likeness of any thing that is in heaven above, or that is in the earth beneath, or that is in the water under the earth:
5 Thou shalt not bow down thyself to them, nor serve them: for I Yahweh thy Elohim am a jealous El, visiting the iniquity of the fathers upon the children unto the third and fourth generation of

them that hate me;
6 And shewing mercy unto thousands of them that
love me, and keep my commandments.

Yahweh said the people are corrupted.

Exodus 32:7-10
7 And Yahweh said unto Moses, Go, get thee down;
for thy people, which thou broughtest out of the
land of Egypt, have corrupted themselves:
8 They have turned aside quickly out of the way
which I commanded them: they have made them a
molten calf, and have worshipped it, and have
sacrificed thereunto, and said, These be thy
elohim, O Israel, which have brought thee up out of
the land of Egypt.
9 And Yahweh said unto Moses, I have seen this
people, and, behold, it is a stiff-necked people:
10 Now therefore let me alone, that my wrath may
wax hot against them, and that I may consume
them: and I will make of thee a great nation.

And Yahweh was about to destroy them all,
but Moses interceded on their behalf.

Exodus 32:11-14
11 And Moses besought Yahweh his Elohim, and
said, Yahweh, why doth thy wrath wax hot against
thy people, which thou hast brought forth out of the
land of Egypt with great power, and with a mighty
hand?
12 Wherefore should the Egyptians speak, and

say, For mischief did he bring them out, to slay them in the mountains, and to consume them from the face of the earth? Turn from thy fierce wrath, and repent of this evil against thy people.

13 Remember Abraham, Isaac, and Israel, thy servants, to whom thou swarest by thine own self, and saidst unto them, I will multiply your seed as the stars of heaven, and all this land that I have spoken of will I give unto your seed, and they shall inherit it for ever.

14 And Yahweh repented of the evil which he thought to do unto his people.

Look what Moses did next.

Exodus 32:15-19
15 And Moses turned, and went down from the mount, and the two tables of the testimony were in his hand: the tables were written on both their sides; on the one side and on the other were they written.

16 And the tables were the work of Elohim, and the writing was the writing of Elohim, graven upon the tables.

17 And when Joshua heard the noise of the people as they shouted, he said unto Moses, There is a noise of war in the camp.

18 And he said, It is not the voice of them that shout for mastery, neither is it the voice of them that cry for being overcome: but the noise of them that sing do I hear.

19 And it came to pass, as soon as he came nigh

unto the camp, that he saw the calf, and the dancing: and Moses' anger waxed hot, and he cast the tables out of his hands, and brake them beneath the mount.

Moses broke the tablets! And now on to finding grace in the wilderness.

Exodus 33:12-17
12 And Moses said unto Yahweh, See, thou sayest unto me, Bring up this people: and thou hast not let me know whom thou wilt send with me. Yet thou hast said, I know thee by name, and thou hast also found grace#2580 chen *in my sight.*
13 Now therefore, I pray thee, if I have found grace#2580 chen *in thy sight, shew me now thy way, that I may know thee, that I may find grace*#2580 chen *in thy sight: and consider that this nation is thy people.*
14 And he said, **My presence** *shall go with thee, and I will give thee rest.*
15 And he said unto him, If thy presence go not with me, carry us not up hence.
16 For wherein shall it be known here that I and thy people have found grace#2580 chen *in thy sight? is it not in that thou goest with us? so shall we be* **separated***, I and thy people, from all the people that are upon the face of the earth.*
17 And Yahweh said unto Moses, I will do this thing also that thou hast spoken: for thou hast found grace#2580 chen *in my sight, and I know thee by name.*

This is amazing!

#2580 Chen: Protection (chet) of the seed (nun);
Separation (chet) of the seed (nun).

Father's presence goes with Moses and with the children of Israel. Father protects and separates them. If we, like Moses, inquire of Yahweh and go into the tabernacle *(Exodus 33:7-9)*, He will show us His ways, He will lead us with His presence, and He will reveal to the world that we are His people. He knows each of us by name. Thank Him for His presence. Thank Him for His protection. Thank Him for separating us unto Himself.
This is grace!

This is amazing grace!

Psalm 27:7-8 Hear, O Yahweh, when I cry with my voice: have mercy also upon me, and answer me. 8 When thou saidst, Seek ye my face; my heart said unto thee, Thy face, Yahweh, will I seek.

Chapter 14

את

A Great Deception

Matthew 24:4-5
4 And Yeshua answered and said unto them, Take
heed that no man deceive you.
5 For many shall come in my name, saying, I am
Messiah; and shall deceive many.

How many times have we heard, *I am not under*
the law, but under grace? (Rom. 6:14) Which
is often quoted totally out of context. They
purposely leave out what is written before and
after this statement.

Romans 6:12-16 (please look at the entire chapter)
12 Let not sin therefore reign in your mortal body,
that ye should obey it in the lusts thereof.
13 Neither yield ye your members as instruments
of unrighteousness unto sin: but yield yourselves
unto Elohim, as those that are alive from the dead,
and your members as instruments of righteousness

unto Elohim.

14 For sin shall not have dominion over you (sin shall not have authority or rule over you)*: **for ye are not under the law, but under grace**.*

15 What then? shall we sin, because we are not under the law, but under grace? Elohim forbid.

16 Know ye not, that to whom ye yield yourselves servants to obey, his servants ye are to whom ye obey; whether of sin unto death, or of obedience unto righteousness?

Yeshua died so sin could be forgiven. He didn't die so we could sin. How insulting this must be to the Father and to the Son that we have taken the seriousness of Yeshua's sacrifice and reduced it to a level that makes a mockery of Him. His sacrifice has been interpreted to mean that it is ok to sin because we are under grace. It's all under the blood.

But is that true? Grace is **available** to all but it **does not apply** to all.

Could Yeshua be warning us in *Matthew 24:4-5* that there will be *many* who will come in His name, the name of Messiah, the Anointed One, and will teach that *grace applies to all* and will deceive many? The *many* will no longer teach about the Law and sin *(sin is lawlessness)*, and the need for repentance.

Without the Law, there is no understanding of Yahweh's holiness. Without the understanding of Yahweh's holiness, there is no perception of how wicked and unholy we are. Without the perception of how wicked and unholy we are, there is no acknowledgment of sin. Without the acknowledgment of sin, there is no need for repentance. Without repentance, there is no salvation. Without salvation, there is no Yeshua. Without Yeshua, there is no faith.

Without faith, there is no grace!

Jude 1:3-4
3 Beloved, when I gave all diligence to write unto you of the common salvation, it was needful for me to write unto you, and exhort you that ye should earnestly contend for the faith#4102 which was once delivered unto the saints.
4 For there are certain men crept in unawares, who were before of old ordained to this condemnation, impious men, turning the grace of our Elohim into lasciviousness, and denying the only Master Yahweh, and our Master Yeshua Messiah.

The following Scripture has brought much confusion and with confusion comes deception.

Titus 2:11-14
*11 For the grace#5485 (#2580 chen) of Elohim that bringeth salvation **hath appeared to all men**,*
12 Teaching us that, denying impiety and worldly lusts, we should live soberly, righteously, and piously, in this present world;
13 Looking for that blessed hope, and the glorious

appearing of the great Elohim and our Saviour Yeshua Messiah;
14 Who gave himself for us, that he might redeem us from all iniquity, and purify unto himself a peculiar people, zealous of good works.

A subtle shift has happened. *Grace has appeared to all* is being taught as *grace applies to all* and has led and will continue to lead many to believe they can live like the world *(like all the other nations)* and still have access to grace and therefore, still be saved. **But this is not so. This is a great deception.** Grace only applies to those who have faith.

Ephesians 2:8 For by grace are ye saved through faith;

Those who have Yeshua and have been separated from the world and are secured with and being led by His Spirit have grace. Yes, *all* those who have faith, the faith of Yeshua, have access to grace and they will not be judged by the Law. But not *all* have faith.

2Thessalonians 3:2-3
2 And that we may be delivered from unreasonable and wicked men: for all men have not faith#4102.
3 But the Master is faithful, who shall stablish you, and keep you from evil.

Those who lack faith, lack Yeshua. They lack Yeshua because they lack the Word. They lack the Word because Yeshua is the Word. This is an endless cycle. They lack faith, they lack Yeshua, they lack the Word. They lack the Word, they lack Yeshua, they lack faith, repeat.

Yeshua is the Word.

John 1:1 In the beginning was the Word, and the Word was with Elohim, and the Word was Elohim.

Faith comes by hearing the Word.

Romans 10:17 So then faith#4102 cometh by hearing, and hearing by the word of Elohim.

If one does not have faith, then grace does not apply to them and they will be judged by the Law.

Want grace? ...Then find Faith.

John 14:4-6
4 And wither I go ye know, and the way ye know.
5 Thomas saith unto him, Master, we know not whither thou goest; and how can we know the way?
6 Yeshua saith unto him, I am the way, the truth, and the life: no man cometh unto the Father, but by me.

Why the Deception?

The problem with deception is that one doesn't know they are deceived, otherwise it wouldn't be deception. Someone can believe a falsity so earnestly, they are willing to stake their eternity on it. And yet even with all their zeal, this falsity will still be untrue.

2Timothy 3:13 But evil#4190 *ponéros: toilsome, bad; evil, wicked, malicious, slothful men*#444 *anthrópos: a man, human, mankind and seducers*#1114 *goés: a wailer, a sorcerer, a swindler; deceiver, imposter shall wax worse and worse, deceiving*#4105 *planaó: to cause to wander, wander; go astray, get off course, deceive, and being deceived*#4105 *planaó: to cause to wander, wander; go astray, get off course, deceive.*

Deception can sometimes come from simply a lack of knowledge, but more often than not, it will come from those who have *erred from the faith.* *(1Timothy 6:10)*

1Timothy 6:9-12
9 But they that will be rich fall into temptation and a snare, and into many foolish and hurtful lusts, which drown men in destruction and perdition.
10 For the love of money is the root of all evil: which while some coveted after, they have erred from the faith#4102*, and pierced themselves through with many sorrows.*
11 But thou, O man of Elohim, flee these things; and follow after righteousness, piety, faith#4102*,*

love, patience, meekness.
12 Fight the good fight of faith#4102*, lay hold on eternal life*#2222 zóé*, whereunto thou art also called, and hast professed a good profession before many witnesses.*

There will be those who have earned the title *prosperity preacher* and other religious leaders, whose actions *(deceiving and being deceived 2Tim. 3:13)* stem from *the love of money. (1Tim. 6:10)* And in an effort to keep those they have influence over giving their time and money, they will hold back truth, compromise truth, or simply make up truth, so as to not offend anyone. After all, convicting anyone of their sin could have financial implications.

2Timothy 4:2-5
2 Preach the word; be instant in season, out of season; reprove, rebuke, exhort with all longsuffering and doctrine.
3 For the time will come when they will not endure sound doctrine; but after their own lusts shall they heap to themselves teachers, having itching ears;
4 And they shall turn away their ears from the truth, and shall be turned unto fables.
5 But watch thou in all things, endure afflictions, do the work of an evangelist, make full proof of thy ministry.

Dear Beloved,

Love the Word of Elohim. Love His instructions, His teachings, His Law, His Torah. Don't let your heart grow cold to the things of Yahweh. Seek Him while He may be found. Call upon Him while He is near. Don't compromise on your commitment to follow His instructions. Yes, you will be criticized and ridiculed for doing so, but don't grow weary.

Matthew 24:9-13
9 Then shall they deliver you up to be afflicted, and shall kill you: and ye shall be hated of all nations for my name's sake.
10 And then shall many be offended, and shall betray one another, and shall hate one another.
11 And many false prophets shall rise, and shall deceive many.
12 And because iniquity#458 *anomia: lawlessness; without law shall abound, the love of many shall wax cold.*
13 But he that shall endure unto the end, the same shall be saved.

In the next chapter, we will take a look at *John 10:10*. It will give us a great example of how man, through the influence of flesh and the devil, can twist the Scriptures to say something that upon closer examination, isn't there.

Chapter 15

את

So Who is the Thief?

*John 10:10 The **thief***#2812 kleptés: a thief *cometh not, but for to steal*#2813 kleptó: to steal*, and to kill*#2380 thuó: to offer, sacrifice*, and to destroy*#622 apollumi: to destroy, destroy utterly*: I am come that they might have life*#2222 zóé: life*, and that they might have it more abundantly*#4053 perissos: abundant*.*

This passage of Scripture is most commonly *misquoted* as:

The **enemy** comes to steal and to kill and to destroy...or **Satan** comes to steal and to kill and to destroy...or the **devil** comes to steal and to kill and to destroy...

But the word for thief comes from the Greek word kleptes, which means a thief. Kleptomaniac is derived from this word.

Yeshua was addressing *the religious leaders.*

John 9:40-41
(Yeshua heals a man born blind John 9:1-41)
40 And some of the Pharisees which were with him heard these words, and said unto him, Are we blind also?
41 Yeshua said unto them, If ye were blind, ye should have no sin: but now ye say, We see; therefore your sin remaineth.

John 10:1 (This is a continuation from John 9)
(Yeshua still speaking to *the religious leaders*)
1 Verily#281 amén: truly, *verily*#281, *I say unto you, He that entereth not by the door*#2374 thura: a door *into the sheepfold, but climbeth up some other way, that same is a thief*#2812 kleptés: a thief *and a robber*#3027 léstés: a robber.

He that *entereth not by the door* is both *a thief* and *a robber.*

John 10:2-3
2 But he that entereth in by the door#2374 thura: a door *is the **shepherd** of the sheep.*
3 To him the porter#2377 thuróros: a doorkeeper *openeth; and the sheep hear his voice: and he calleth his own sheep by name, and leadeth them out.*

Porter also comes from the word guardian. Someone who guards the door. The doorkeeper (*gatekeeper or watchman*) is looking for the

114

Shepherd. The doorkeeper is not the Shepherd. The doorkeeper's job is to keep watch and when he sees the Shepherd, he opens the door. He only opens the door to the Shepherd. And when he opens the door *the sheep hear his voice; and he calleth his own sheep by name, and leadeth them out. (John 10:3)* The sheep follow the Shepherd. They do not follow the doorkeeper.

John 10:4-6
4 And when he putteth forth his own sheep, he goeth before them, and the sheep follow him: for they know his voice.
5 And a stranger#245 allotrios: belonging to another *will they not follow, but will flee from him: for they know not the voice of strangers*#245 allotrios: belonging to another.
6 This parable spake Yeshua unto them: but they understood not what things they were which he spake unto them.

Yeshua has to add further clarification to His remarks because the Pharisees did not understand Him. So He goes on to explain that He is not only the Shepherd of the sheep that goes in through the door but that He is also the door.

John 10:7-10
7 Then said Yeshua unto them again, Verily, verily, I say unto you, I am the door#2374 thura: a door *of the sheep.*
8 All that ever came before me are thieves#2812 kleptés: a thief *and robbers*#3027 léstés: a robber: *but the sheep did*

not hear them.

9 I am the door#2374 thura: a door: by me if any man enter in, he shall be saved, and shall go in and out, and find pasture.

10 *The thief#2812 kleptés: a thief cometh not, but for to steal#2813 kleptó: to steal, and to kill#2380 thuo: to offer, sacrifice, and to destroy#622 apollumi: to destroy, destroy utterly: I am come that they might have life#2222 zóé: life, and that they might have it more abundantly#4053 perissos: abundant.*

Yeshua was talking about eternal life, *he shall be saved. (John 10:9)* He was not talking about material possessions.

Luke 12:15 And he said unto them, Take heed, and beware of covetousness: for a man's life#2222 zóé: life consisteth not in the abundance of the things which he possesseth.

John 11:25-26 Yeshua said unto her, I am the resurrection, and the life#2222 zóé: life: he that believeth in me, though he were dead, yet shall he live: 26 And whosoever liveth and believeth in me shall never die...

John 10:11-13 (continuing on)
11 I am the good shepherd: the good shepherd giveth his life for the sheep.
12 But he that is an hireling#3411 misthótos: hired, a hired servant, and not the shepherd, whose own the sheep are not, seeth the wolf coming, and leaveth the

sheep, and fleeth: and the wolf catcheth#726 *harpapó:* to seize, catch up, snatch away, obtain by robbery *them, and scattereth*#4650 *skorpizó: to scatter, disperse the sheep.*

(the wolf: false prophet Mat.7:15)
13 The hireling#3411 *misthótos: hired, a hired servant fleeth, because he is an hireling*#3411 *misthótos: hired, a hired servant, and careth not for the sheep.*

1Peter 5:2-4 Feed the flock of Elohim which is among you, taking the oversight thereof, not by constraint, but willingly; not for filthy lucre, but of a ready mind; 3 Neither as being masters over#2634 *katakurieuo: I exercise authority over, overpower those entrusted to you, but being examples to the flock. 4 And when the chief Shepherd shall appear, ye shall receive a crown of glory that fadeth not away.*

John 10:14-16 (continuing on)
14 I am the good shepherd, and know my sheep, and am known of mine.
15 As the Father knoweth me, even so know I the Father: and I lay down my life for the sheep.
16 And other sheep I have, which are not of this fold: them also I must bring, and they shall hear my voice; and there shall be one fold, and one shepherd.

The thief, the robber, the stranger, and the hireling are all one and the same person. Did you get that? The thief is a person. It is not the enemy, satan, or the devil, even though this person may be being influenced by the devil.

117

Ephesians 6:12 For we wrestle not against flesh and blood...

Be alert! This person has found a way into the sheepfold, but they have found a way in that is not by the door.

This person is anyone who holds an influential position and uses their position to lead the sheep astray, to steal from the sheep, to kill the sheep, to destroy the sheep and leave the sheep. This person cares not for the sheep. It is those who have no problem with taking money from an elderly woman who has lost her husband and is on a fixed income such as social security or disability, or from a single mom who is doing everything she can to provide for her children, or from the poor and the desperate who don't know where they are going to get their next meal. They lack any conviction when they take money from the hungry, the thirsty, the stranger, the naked, the sick, and the prisoner. *(Matthew 25:31-40)*

It is extremely important to see this. It has been and will continue to be the thief *(an actual person)* that has found a way inside the body that will fleece and devour the sheep. It will be the ones that have some degree of power, control, and influence. These thieves steal from the poor, the fatherless, the widow, and the alien. They kill hopes and dreams and destroy lives with their false teachings, their lies, and their manipulation of men and Scripture. Sure, a single individual or even a couple within the Ekklésia can cause some harm to the body, but it is these thieves, robbers, strangers, and hirelings that are the most destructive. Because they care not for the sheep, at the first sign of danger, they will run without even warning the flock. Because to them, as the flock is being destroyed and devoured, it gives them more time to escape.

Don't be deceived by those who use the Word of Elohim for financial gain. Beloved, you know who they are and you know when they are doing it. You have the Spirit, and you know when something isn't right.

The Shepherd and The Door

Yeshua used an analogy of a shepherd and a door and He stated that He is both.

First, let us take a look at the Door.

The door acts as an entrance and an exit, *if any man enter in, he shall be saved, and shall go in and out, and find pasture. (John 10:9)*

Second, let us take a look at the Shepherd.

The Shepherd leads the flock, *he calleth his own sheep by name, and leadeth them out. (John 10:3)* The Shepherd gives his life for the flock, *I am the good shepherd: the good shepherd giveth his life for the sheep. (John 10:11)*

The Shepherd knows the sheep, *I am the good shepherd, and know my sheep, and am known of mine. (John 10:14)*

If Yeshua is both the Shepherd and the Door, then there must be a false shepherd (*they look like a shepherd*) and a counterfeit door (*the wrong entrance*).

The false shepherd is someone who gets in through other means. *Verily, verily, I say unto you, He that entereth not by the door into the sheepfold, but climbeth up some other way, that same is a thief and a robber. (John 10:1)*

The counterfeit door is an entrance, but it is the wrong entrance (believing there are many ways to be saved). *I am the door: by me if any man enter in, he shall be saved, and shall go in and out, and find pasture. The thief cometh not, but for to steal, and to kill, and to destroy: I am come that they might have life*#2222 zóé: life*, and that they might have it more abundantly. (John 10:9-10)*

Beware of those who preach a false faith *(That all one has to do is believe. Really? The devil believes and is he saved?).* And who preach a false grace *(No need to keep the commandments, it's all covered by the blood. Really? Yeshua said if we love Him, we will keep His commandments).* Watch out! For they are *thieves* and they are *robbers*.

How to Spot the Thief

You Shall Know Them by Their Fruit

Matthew 7:15 Beware of false prophets (not from Yahweh), *which come to you in sheep's clothing* (they look like a fellow believer), *but inwardly* (in their heart) *they are ravening*#727 harpax: rapacious, ravenous; a robber, an extortioner (from #726 harpapó: to seize, catch up, snatch away, obtain by robbery) *wolves.*

Rapacious: excessively grasping or covetous.
Ravenous: very eager or greedy for food,
satisfaction, or gratification.
Extortion: the practice of obtaining something,
especially money, through force or threats.

Matthew 7:16-20
16 Ye shall know them by their fruits. Do men gather grapes of thorns, or figs of thistles?
17 Even so every good tree bringeth forth#4160 poieó: to make, do; manufacture, construct (produce) *good fruit; but a corrupt tree bringeth forth*#4160 poieó *evil fruit.*
18 A good tree cannot bring forth#4160 poieó *evil fruit, neither can a corrupt tree bring forth*#4160 poieó *good fruit.*
19 Every tree that bringeth not forth#4160 poieó *good fruit is hewn down, and cast into the fire.*
20 Wherefore by their fruits ye shall know them.

How do you recognize a true prophet or a fellow brother or sister in Messiah? You recognize them, <u>not</u> by what they **say**, but by what they **produce**. By the fruit they make, manufacture, construct, and produce, you will recognize them.

We must beware of the thief because when they are exposed, they will try to kill any fruit that Yahweh has begun to produce in your life. They will revile you, persecute you, and will try to destroy you by spewing all sorts of untruths about you. But remember what Yeshua said:

Matthew 5:11-12
11 Blessed are ye, when men shall revile you, and persecute you, and shall say all manner of evil against you falsely, for my sake.
12 Rejoice, and be exceeding glad: for great is your reward in heaven: for so persecuted they the prophets which were before you.

Yeshua warned us, so there will be *thieves*. As part of the sheepfold, we must do whatever we can to protect others within the fold. We should be willing to stand up for the weakest among us and not let these *thieves* fleece the sheep.

Chapter 16

את

Will Yeshua Find Faith?

Yeshua asked, *"When the Son of man cometh, shall he find faith on the earth?"* Why did He ask this?

Luke 18:1-8
1 And he spake a parable unto them to this end, that men ought[# 1163: dei: it is necessary] always to pray, and not to faint[# 1573 ekkakeó: faint, be weary];
2 Saying, There was in a city a judge, which feared not Elohim, neither regarded man:
3 And there was a widow in that city; and she came unto him, saying, Avenge me of mine adversary.
4 And he would not for a while: but afterward he said within himself, Though I fear not Elohim, nor regard man;
5 Yet because this widow troubleth me, I will

avenge her, lest by her continual coming she weary me.
6 And the Master said, Hear what the unjust judge saith.
7 And shall not Elohim avenge his own elect, which cry day and night unto him, though he bear long with them?
8 I tell you that he will avenge them speedily. Nevertheless when the Son of man cometh, shall he find#2147 heuriskó: to find *faith*#4102 *on the earth?*

Did He ask this because a time will come when men will have grown weary and will have lost faith? A time when faith, not belief, but emunah, will be hard to find?

Matthew 24:13 But he that shall endure unto the end, the same shall be saved.

A time when they will doubt Yeshua.

2Peter 3:3-4
3 Knowing this first, that there shall come in the last days scoffers, walking after their own lusts,
4 And saying, Where is the promise of his coming? for since the fathers fell asleep, all things continue as they were from the beginning of the creation.

A time when they will be distracted by the world.

Matthew 24:37-39
37 But as the days of Noah were, so shall also the

coming of the Son of man be.
38 For as in the days that were before the flood they were eating and drinking, marrying and giving in marriage, until the day that Noah entered into the ark,
39 And knew not until the flood came, and took them all#537 hapas: all, the whole *away; so shall also the coming of the Son of man be.*

Who is the *ALL* Yeshua is referring to?

Genesis 7:21-23
21 And all flesh died that moved upon the earth, both of fowl, and of cattle, and of beast, and of every creeping thing that creepeth upon the earth, and every man:
22 All in whose nostrils was the breath of life, of all that was in the dry land, died.
23 And every living substance was destroyed which was upon the face of the ground, both man, and cattle, and the creeping things, and the fowl of the heaven; and they were destroyed from the earth: and Noah only remained alive, and they that were with him in the ark.

Remember, out of all flesh on earth, Noah was the only one that *found grace in the eyes of Yahweh. (Gen. 6:8) He* was the only one Yahweh had protected and separated unto Himself. Yeshua said, *"And knew not until the flood came, and took them all*#537 hapas: all, the whole *away; so shall also the coming of the Son of man be." (Matthew 24:39)*

125

The *ALL* that Yeshua was referring to will be all those who will not have faith. They will not know the true meaning of faith, and as such, will not have it. The *ALL* who say that faith is wishful thinking or that faith is belief. Faith is not a thought. Faith is a person. Faith is Yeshua. This is why He asked, *"When the Son of man cometh, shall He find faith on the earth?" (Luke 18:8)* When He comes, He will be looking for faith. Will He find it in you?

Finding Faith in an Unlikely Place

My Sister and my brother, let me give you a word of encouragement. If Father has called you to do something for the Kingdom, do it. Don't let man stop you and don't let him slow you down. You see, sinful man *(mankind)*, in his fallen state, is always seeking to control other men. They want the power and authority to either approve or disapprove of what you do. But Father is the One who approves.

It doesn't matter where you come from or what you've done. If He has called you and has put His faith in you, then you must listen, obey, and be a witness of Yeshua on the earth. When you leave your former way of life and become bold in Messiah, man will doubt that you've changed and will find it highly unlikely. But, Yahweh does miracles! He can put faith into an unlikely place!

Matthew 8:5-13
*5 And when Yeshua was entered into Capernaum,
there came unto him a centurion*#1543 *hekatontarchés: a
centurion, a captain of 100 men, a centurion of the Roman army*,
beseeching him,
*6 And saying, Master, my servant lieth at home
sick of the palsy, grievously tormented.*
*7 And Yeshua saith unto him, I will come and heal
him.*
*8 The centurion answered and said, Master, I am
not worthy*#2425 *hikanos: sufficient, fit that thou shouldest
come under*#5259 *hupo: by, under my roof: but speak the
word only, and my servant shall be healed.*
9 For I am a man under#5259 *hupo: by, under
authority*#1849 *exousia: power to act, authority, having soldiers
under me: and I say to this man, Go, and he goeth;
and to another, Come, and he cometh; and to my
servant, Do this, and he doeth it.*
*10 When Yeshua heard it, he marvelled, and said
to them that followed, Verily*#281 *amén: truly I say unto
you, I have not* **found**#2147 *heuriskó: to find so great*#5118
tosoutos: so great, so much, so many **faith**#4102*, no, not in Israel.*
*11 And I say unto you, That many shall come from
the east and west, and shall sit down*#347 *anaklinó: to
lay upon, lay down, to lie back; recline with Abraham, and Isaac,
and Jacob, in the kingdom of heaven.*
*12 But the children of the kingdom shall be cast out
into outer darkness: there shall be weeping and
gnashing of teeth.*
*13 And Yeshua said unto the centurion, Go thy
way; and as thou hast believed* (Yeshua defines
this belief as faith in Matthew 8:10), *so be it done*

unto thee. And his servant was healed in the selfsame hour.

We should note this is not about Yeshua giving the approval of a hierarchal structure within the Ekklésia, within the body of Messiah, because he speaks against this.

Matthew 20:25-28
25 But Yeshua called them unto him, and said, Ye know that the princes#758 *archón: ruler, chief of the Gentiles exercise dominion*#2634 *katakurieuo: I exercise authority over, overpower over them, and they that are great exercise authority*#2715 *katexousiazó: to exercise authority over upon them.*
26 But it shall not be so among you: but whosoever will be great among you, let him be your minister#1249 *diakonos: a servant, minister;*
27 And whosoever will be chief among you, let him be your servant#1401 *doulos: a slave:*
28 Even as the Son of man came not to be ministered#1247 *diakoneó: to serve, minister unto, but to minister*#1247 *diakoneó: to serve, minister, and to give his life a ransom for many.*

We should also note that Yeshua equates this centurion's response, a man under Gentile rulership, equivalent to one having great faith and likened to one of the many coming *from the east and west, and shall recline with Abraham, and Isaac, and Jacob, in the kingdom of heaven (Matthew 8:11).* while the children of the kingdom *shall be cast out into outer darkness (Matthew 8:12).* Yeshua was able to find faith in someone who was not a part of Israel so even the Gentiles can find faith.

Remember faith comes from Elohim and is always Yahweh's divine persuasion.

Matthew 16:16-17
16 And Simon Peter answered and said, Thou are the Messiah, the Son of the living Elohim.
17 And Yeshua answered and said unto him, Blessed art thou, Simon Bar-jona: for flesh and blood hath not revealed it unto thee, but my Father which is in heaven.

What did this centurion see in Yeshua? This centurion, a man of high ranking, had the authority to give orders, but he also took orders from those above him in ranking. And yet he asked Yeshua, a civilian, someone who had no ranking and absolutely no authority in the Roman army, to *speak the word only and my servant shall be healed (Matthew 8:8).* Yahweh had revealed to this centurion that Yeshua had supreme authority.

Matthew 28:18-20
18 And Yeshua came and spake unto them, saying, All power# 1849 exousia: power to act, authority is given unto me in heaven and in earth.
19 Go ye therefore, and teach all nations, baptizing them in the name of the Father, and of the Son, and of the Spirit:

20 Teaching them to observe all things whatsoever I have commanded you: and, lo, I am with you always, even unto the end of the world. Amen.

The centurion said I am not *fit* or I am not *sufficient* to have you come under my roof because he recognized the authority he had in his own home, under his own roof. It would have been completely out of order for Yeshua, the one will *all* authority, to come into his home and be placed *under authority*. This hierarchal structure Yeshua said is the way of the Gentiles, *(Mat. 20:25)* and should not be the way for those in the Kingdom. He commanded that the *children of the kingdom* be as servants and slaves.

Matthew 20:26 But it shall not be so among you: but whosoever will be great among you, let him be your minister#1249 *diakonos: a servant, minister; 27 And whosoever will be chief among you, let him be your servant*#1401 *doulos: a slave:*

Because there is already one Master and King.

1Timothy 6:13-16
13 I give thee charge in the sight of Elohim, who quickeneth all things, and before Messiah Yeshua, who before Pontius Pilate witnessed a good confession;
14 That thou keep this commandment without spot, unrebukeable, until the appearing of our Master Yeshua Messiah:

15 Which in his times he shall show, who is the blessed and only Potentate#1413 dunastés: a ruler, a potentate, the King of kings, and Master of masters;
16 Who only hath immortality, dwelling in the light which no man can approach unto; whom no man hath seen, nor can see: to whom be honour and power everlasting. Amen.

We have grown accustomed to believing this example is about authority, but as we have now taken a much deeper look, we discover it is more about finding faith in an unlikely place. Yeshua found faith in a centurion, a Gentile. And this centurion found faith in a common man, or so he thought.

Psalm 42:1-2 As the hart panteth after the water brooks, so panteth my soul after thee, O Elohim. 2 My soul thirsteth for Elohim, for the living Elohim: when shall I come and appear before Elohim?

Chapter 17

את

The Strait Gate

Yes, we must strive to enter in at the strait gate, but first, we must find it.

Find the Strait Gate

Matthew 7:13-14
13 Enter ye in at the strait#4728 stenos: narrow, strait *gate: for wide is the gate, and broad is the way, that leadeth to destruction, and many there be which go in thereat:*
14 Because strait#4728 stenos: narrow, strait *is the gate, and narrow*#2346 thlibó: to press, afflict *is the way, which leadeth unto life, and few there be that find it.*

Unfortunately, many won't find the strait gate and the narrow way.

Luke 13:23-25
23 Then said one unto him, Master, are there few

that be saved? And he said unto them,
24 Strive#75 agónizomai: to contend for a prize, struggle *to enter in at the strait*#4728 stenos: narrow, strait *gate: for many, I say unto you, will seek to enter in, and shall not be able.*
25 When once the Master of the house is risen up, and hath shut to the door, and ye begin to stand without, and to knock at the door, saying, Master, Master, open unto us; and he shall answer and say unto you, **I know you not** *whence ye are:* (What a terrifying and painful thing to hear the Master say, "I know you not".)

There will be *many* who believe in Yeshua and yet are *workers of iniquity.*

Luke 13:26-27
26 Then shall ye begin to say, We have eaten and drunk in thy presence, and thou hast taught in our streets.
27 But he shall say, I tell you, I know you not whence ye are; depart from me, all ye workers of iniquity#93 adikia: injustice, unrighteousness.

Many will not be able to find the strait gate *(Yeshua is the strait gate)* nor find the narrow way *(Yeshua is the narrow way),* even though they will have convinced themselves and convinced others that they have. They will have been led astray and will have followed the false shepherd and will have gone through the counterfeit door.

Matthew 7:21-23
21 Not every one that saith unto me, Master, Master, shall enter into the kingdom of heaven; but he that doeth the will of my Father which is in heaven.
22 Many will say to me in that day, Master, Master, have we not prophesied in thy name? and in thy name have cast out devils? and in thy name done many wonderful works?
23 And then will I profess unto them, I never knew you: depart from me, ye that work iniquity[#458] *anomia: lawlessness; without law*.

From the outside, *many* will look like they have found the Way. *Yeshua saith unto him, I am the way, the truth, and the life: no man cometh unto the Father, but by me. (John 14:6) Many* will mistakenly think that Yahweh approves of their behavior because while they are practicing lawlessness, they are able to prophesy, cast out demons, and do many wonderful works. And yet Yeshua said, *"I never knew you."* (Mat. 7:23) If we want to find the strait gate and the narrow way, we must hear the words of Yeshua and do them.

Matthew 7:24-27
24 Therefore whosoever heareth these sayings of mine, and doeth them, I will liken him unto a wise man, which built his house upon a rock:
25 And the rain descended, and the floods came, and the winds blew, and beat upon that house; and it fell not: for it was founded upon a rock.

26 And every one that heareth these sayings of mine, and doeth them not, shall be likened unto a foolish man, which built his house upon the sand: 27 And the rain descended, and the floods came, and the winds blew, and beat upon that house; and it fell: and great was the fall of it.

Whatever you build, build it upon "hearing" and "doing". Build it upon the foundation of His Words. Because if we accept His Word as truth, then we know what is yet to come:

1Peter 4:17-18
17 For the time is come that judgment must begin at the house of Elohim: and if it first begin at us, what shall the end be of them that obey not the gospel of Elohim.
18 And if the righteous scarcely be saved, where shall the unrighteous and the sinner appear?

Psalm 11:3-5
3 If the foundations be destroyed, what can the righteous do?
4 Yahweh is in his holy temple, Yahweh's throne is in heaven: his eyes behold, his eyelids try, the children of men.
5 Yahweh trieth the righteous: but the wicked and him that loveth violence his soul hateth.

Are you striving to find the strait gate? Meaning: Are you urgently and eagerly looking for it? It is likened to finding a needle in a haystack.

You have to concentrate and you have to focus. It requires effort. You have to be careful not to overlook it as you sort through the haystack, or accidentally throw it out with the straw. Give it everything you've got. Find the needle. Find the strait gate. Find Yeshua. *And few there be that find it (Matthew 7:14).*

Not finding it is easy. In fact, it doesn't require any effort at all. *For wide is the gate and broad is the way, that leadeth to destruction, and many there be which go in thereat: (Matthew 7:13)*

Demons Can't Find Faith

James 2:19 Thou believest#4100 pisteuó that there is one Elohim; thou doest well: the devils also believe#4100 pisteuó, and tremble.

Yes, satan and his demons believe and even tremble, but they cannot find faith. Faith is Yahweh's divine persuasion and He only gives this to His children. As His children, we must go beyond the belief and the trembling that demons have. We are called to have the type of faith that when troubles, or persecutions, or sufferings, or trials, or temptations come, we can stand and not be moved. This type of faith can make the most ordinary person do extraordinary things for the Kingdom of Elohim.

John 1:12-13
12 But as many as received him, to them gave he

power#1849 *exousia: power to act, authority, delegated power* **to become the sons of Elohim,** *even to them that believe*#4100 *pisteuó on his name:*
13 Which were born, not of blood, nor of the will of the flesh, nor of the will of man, but of Elohim.

Satan and his demons *can never become* Sons of Elohim. It's no wonder why they hate man. And as a result, they will come up with all sorts of schemes to keep man from becoming Sons of Elohim. They will try to keep man from finding the Way, the Truth, and the Life; to keep man from finding Yeshua, to keep man from finding Faith. And as evident in the world today, they have been very successful at it.

Chapter 18

את

A Grain of Faith

(Small Faith vs. Little Faith)

On many occasions, Yeshua told his disciples they have little faith. In *Matthew 17:20* and *Luke 17:6* He used a mustard seed, one of the tiniest seeds, to illustrate faith.

Matthew 17:20 And Yeshua said unto them, Because of your little faith#3640 oligopistis: of **little faith***: for verily I say unto you, If ye have faith*#4102 pistis *as a grain*#2848 kokkos: a grain, a kernel, seed *of mustard seed, ye shall say unto this mountain, Remove hence to yonder place; and it shall remove; and nothing shall be impossible unto you.*

Yes, we see Yeshua telling His disciples that their faith was little. But does that mean He was saying that their faith was small? Smaller than a mustard seed? Or, was He giving them an illustration of something much deeper?

Matthew 13:31-32
31 Another parable put he forth unto them, saying, The kingdom of heaven is like to a grain#2848 kokkos: a grain, kernel, seed *of mustard seed, which a man took and sowed in his field:*
32 Which indeed is the least#3398 mikros: **small**, little *of all seeds: but when it is grown, it is the greatest*#3173 megas: **great** *among herbs, and becometh a tree, so that the birds of the air come and lodge in the branches thereof.*

It's not so much that their faith was small, **but rather that their faith was little**. Yeshua said, *"If ye have faith as a grain of mustard" (Mat. 17:20)*. He is equating faith to grain. *"Which a man took and sowed in his field...but when it is grown, it is the greatest" (Mat. 13:31-32)*.

Their faith was little. **Little faith is really unbelief** *(disguised as doubt)*. But when someone has small faith, it is really His faith. And even though it may not be fully grown, it is still His faith and His faith is great!

When we trust in our own faith, we are really trusting in our own ability to believe. Trusting in our own ability to believe, will cause us to doubt. We will ask ourselves, "Do I have enough faith?" This puts the focus of our attention on *self* instead of where it should be, on Yeshua.

Those that have become children of Elohim are secured by the blood. They are filled with and are being led by the Spirit. They are learning the difference between belief and faith. They are learning the difference between little faith and small faith. Yes, believe in Yeshua. But also have the faith of Yeshua. His faith is perfect! And His faith moves mountains! *(Matthew 17:20)*

Hebrews 12:2 Looking unto Yeshua the author and finisher of our faith...

What If I Doubt?
(What If I Have Little Faith?)

Mark 9:19-24
19 He answered him, and saith, O faithless#571 apistos: unbelieving *generation, how long shall I be with you? how long shall I suffer you? bring him unto me.*
20 And they brought him unto him: and when he saw him, straightway the spirit tare him; and he fell on the ground, and wallowed foaming.
21 And he asked his father, How long is it ago since this came unto him? And he said, Of a child.
22 And ofttimes it hath cast him into the fire, and into the waters, to destroy him: but if thou canst do any thing, have compassion on us, and help us.
23 Yeshua said unto him, If thou canst believe, all things are possible to him that believeth#4100 pisteuó: to believe, entrust (coming from self).

24 And straightway the father of the child cried out, and said with tears, Master, I believe#4100 pisteuó: to believe, entrust (coming from self)*; help thou mine unbelief*#570 apistia: unbelief.

#570 Apistia: unbelief, unfaithfulness *(diso-bedience)*, distrust, faithlessness, disbelief.

This is an extremely important lesson for us today. Unbelief outweighs belief. Yeshua was not misleading this father by implying, *"If only you would believe enough or if only you would have enough faith."* No. He was teaching him that in man's own ability to believe, unbelief will prevail. So, what are we to do?

Overcome Unbelief With Obedience

An easy solution and one that will put an end to unbelief is obedience. When we obey, there is no room for unbelief. Unbelief is simply a lack of trust. Yahweh tells us to do this or to not do that, but we don't trust that He will take care of us and that He knows what is best. And the end result is unbelief. Knowing that unbelief is simply a lack of trust will teach us that it is something we can overcome. We can overcome unbelief by trusting Yahweh. And trusting Yahweh requires obedience.

Hebrews 3:18-19
18 And to whom sware he that they should not enter into his rest, but to them that believeth not[#544]
apeitheó: to disobey, rebel?

19 So we see that they could not enter in because of unbelief[#570 apistia].

So, when you find yourself in a state of unbelief, masquerading itself as doubt, try obedience. Try trusting in Yahweh. Try trusting in Yeshua and living by faith.

142

Live By Faith

Galatians 2:20 I am crucified with Messiah: nevertheless I live; yet not I, but Messiah liveth in me: and the life which I now live in the flesh I live by faith#4102 of the Son of Elohim, who loved me, and gave himself for me.

But most importantly...

Yeshua Remains Faithful

2Timothy 2:13 If we are believe not#569 apisteó: to disbelieve, be faithless, yet he abideth faithful#4103 pistos: faithful, reliable: he cannot deny#720 arneomai: to deny, refuse himself.

If we have the Spirit of Elohim, then we are the children of Elohim and Yeshua lives in us. It is impossible for Yeshua to deny Himself. He remains faithful to Himself. He remains faithful to His faith. It is no longer **you** who remains faithful, it is **Him**. I must say this again, He cannot deny Himself. I hope this takes some of the burden off of you to have great faith. Trust in His faith. *"He abideth faithful!" (2Tim. 2:13)*

*Habakkuk 2:4 ...but the just shall live by **his faith**.*

Philippians 3:7-14 But what things were gain to me, those I counted loss for Messiah. 8 Yea doubtless, and I count all things but loss for the excellency of the knowledge of Messiah Yeshua my Master: for whom I have suffered the loss of all things, and do count them but dung, that I may win Messiah, 9 And be found in him, not having mine own righteousness, which is of the law, but that which is through the faith of Messiah, the righteousness which of is Elohim by faith: 10 That I may know him, and the power of his resurrection, and the fellowship of his sufferings, being made conformable unto his death; 11 If by any means I might attain unto the resurrection of the dead. 12 Not as though I had already attained, either were already perfect: but I follow after, if that I may apprehend that for which also I am apprehended of Messiah Yeshua. 13 Brethren, I count not myself to have apprehended: but this one thing I do, forgetting those things which are behind, and reaching forth unto those things which are before, 14 I press toward the mark for the prize of the high calling of Elohim in Messiah Yeshua.

Chapter 19

את

He Will Reward You

Hebrews 11:6 But without faith it is impossible to please him: for he that cometh to Elohim must believe that he is, and that he is a rewarder of them that diligently seek him.

As I contemplated the above Scripture, I tried to figure out, "What does He reward us with?" Sure, we have been told material possessions, physical health, answered prayers, etc.

Matthew 6:31-33
31 Therefore take no thought, saying, What shall we eat? or, What shall we drink? or, Wherewithal shall we be clothed?
32 (For after all these things do the Gentiles seek:) for your heavenly Father knoweth that ye have need of all these things.
33 But seek ye first the kingdom of Elohim, and his righteousness; and all these things shall be added unto you.

The previous verse is most often taught as: Seek Elohim first and then He will give you stuff. He rewards us with food and drink and clothing and stuff.

Yet, isn't the reward much bigger than that? A reward so much greater than anything that has earthly value? A reward so immeasurable and so vast it is hard for us to comprehend with our little minds?

Jeremiah 29:12-14
12 Then shall ye call upon me, and ye shall go and pray unto me, and I will hearken unto you.
13 And ye shall seek me, and find me, when ye shall search for me with all your heart.
14 And I will be found of you, saith Yahweh...

Did you catch that? When we seek him with all our heart, we will find *HIM*. So to answer the question, "What does He reward us with?"

HE REWARDS US WITH HIMSELF!!!

There is nothing greater than that.

Chapter 20

את

A Final Explanation

For by grace are you saved through faith!
For by *(chen)* are you saved through *(emunah)*!

My hope is that we can now explain the above statement in simple concrete terms; the simplicity that is in Messiah. *(2Cor. 11:3)* It doesn't need to be complex or magical. Let's take a look at Paul.

2Corinthians 12:7-9 ...there was given to me a thorn in the flesh, the messenger of satan to buffet me, lest I should be exalted above measure.
8 For this thing I besought the Master thrice, that it might depart from me.
9 And he said unto me, My grace[#5485 (#2580 chen)] *is sufficient for thee: for my strength*[#1411 dunamis: (miraculous) power, might, strength] *is made perfect in weakness. Most gladly therefore will I rather glory in my infirmities, that the power*[#1411 dunamis] *of Messiah may rest upon me.*

When we insert the abstract Greek meaning of the word grace: *My grace, My kindness, My favor is sufficient for thee,* the average individual would most likely be confused and maybe even disappointed. But not Paul. Why? Because he knew the concrete Hebrew meaning of the word.

"My protection is sufficient for thee."
Wow!

Chen: pictograph of a fence and a seed
Protection of the seed.

Place Paul inside the fence with the fence being Yeshua. Paul was protected by the Father through Yeshua.

The Messiah's miraculous power, might and strength *(strength#1411 dunamis) is made perfect in weakness (2Cor. 12:9).* Paul would rather *glory in* his *infirmities,* so that the Messiah's dunamis (*miraculous power, might, and strength)* might rest upon him.

This is so powerful. When we embrace our weaknesses, the miraculous power of Yeshua rests upon us.

2Corinthians 12:10 Therefore I take pleasure in infirmities, in reproaches, in necessities, in persecutions, in distresses for Messiah's sake: for when I am weak, then am I strong.

Through Yeshua, one gains access to the protection of the Father; one gains access to grace. Through Yeshua, one has escaped being judged by the Law into the judgment that is of Messiah.

Acts 17:31 Because he hath appointed a day, in the which he will judge the world in righteousness by that Man whom he hath ordained; whereof he hath given assurance unto all men, in that he hath raised him from the dead.

So shout this from the rooftops,

"For by grace are you saved through faith."

And when someone asked you, "What does that mean?" Say to them:

"Through Yeshua, you have the protection of the Father. Yeshua's miraculous power, might, and strength rests upon you and He will judge you, not according to the Law, which you broke, but according to Yeshua."

Matthew 5:14-16 Ye are the light of the world. A city that is set on an hill cannot be hid. 15 Neither do men light a candle, and put it under a bushel, but on a candlestick; and it giveth light unto all that are in the house. 16 Let your light so shine before men, that they may see your good works, and glorify your Father which is in heaven.

Chapter 21

את

What's In the Name?

Do we ever stop and wonder if the Father has a name? Did He tell us His name? *(Isa. 42:8 I am Yahweh[#3068] יהוה that is my name...)* Yet we usually refer to Him by His title (God or LORD). The Father's name is made up of four letters known as the Tetragrammaton (consisting of four letters). Unfortunately, His name, which appears thousands of times in the bible has been removed from most translations and replaced with the title LORD. The translators did this in an effort to not misuse the Name, but the end result is we have forgotten that He has a name.

Father does have a name and His name is:

YAHWEH (YHWH)
Spelled Yod, Hey, Waw, Hey

Yod: pictograph of an arm and hand
To work, a deed done, a finished work.

Hey: pictograph of a man with arms raised
Behold, to show, reveal, Spirit, worship.

Waw: pictograph of a tent peg
Nail, firm, secure, join together, becoming bound
(nailed to).

Hey: pictograph of a man with arms raised
Behold, to show, reveal, Spirit, worship.

Meaning: Behold (hey) the hand (yod),
Behold (hey) the nail (waw).
And: The hand (yod) revealed (hey),
The nail (waw) revealed (hey).

We see the Son is in the Father's Name.

Isaiah 53:1-12
1 Who hath believed our report? and to whom is the arm of Yahweh revealed?
2 For he shall grow up before him as a tender plant, and as a root out of a dry ground: he hath no form nor comeliness; and when we shall see him, there is no beauty that we should desire him.
3 He is despised and rejected of men; a man of sorrows, and acquainted with grief: and we hid as it were our faces from him; he was despised, and we esteemed him not.
4 Surely he hath borne our griefs, and carried our sorrows: yet we did esteem him stricken, smitten of Elohim, and afflicted.
5 But he was wounded for our transgressions, he

was bruised for our iniquities: the chastisement of our peace was upon him; and with his stripes we are healed.

6 All we like sheep have gone astray; we have turned every one to his own way; and Yahweh hath laid on him the iniquity of us all.

7 He was oppressed, and he was afflicted, yet he opened not his mouth: he is brought as a lamb to the slaughter, and as a sheep before her shearers is dumb, so he openeth not his mouth.

8 He was taken from prison and from judgment: and who shall declare his generation? for he was cut off out of the land of the living: for the transgression of my people was he stricken.

9 And he made his grave with the wicked, and with the rich in his death; because he had done no violence, neither was any deceit in his mouth.

10 Yet it pleased Yahweh to bruise him; he hath put him to grief: when thou shalt make his soul an offering for sin, he shall see his seed, he shall prolong his days, and the pleasure of Yahweh shall prosper in his hand.

11 He shall see of the travail of his soul, and shall be satisfied: by his knowledge shall my righteous servant justify many; for he shall bear their iniquities.

12 Therefore will I divide him a portion with the great, and he shall divide the spoil with the strong; because he hath poured out his soul unto death: and he was numbered with the transgressors; and he bare the sin of many, and made intercession for the transgressors.

Numbers 6:24-26 Yahweh bless thee, and keep thee: 25 Yahweh make his face shine upon thee, and be gracious unto thee: 26 Yahweh lift up his countenance upon thee, and give thee peace.

Chapter 22

את

A Prayer for the Reader

A Prayer for Faith

Abba Father, in the name of Yeshua, I thank you for mercy. I thank you for grace. I thank you for faith. I thank you for who you are and all that you are. For you are a mighty Elohim. You are bigger than life. You are bigger than death. And you are bigger than everything in between. You are a wonderful and merciful Elohim. And you are worthy.

Abba, I pray for those who have read and who will read this book. I pray that even though it is far from perfect, that in you it would be made perfect, for your Name's sake and for the sake of the reader. Abba, please bless them. Please let them know that you are with them, always guiding them, always comforting them, and always protecting them. Speak to them and let them hear you say, *"This is the way, walk ye in it."*

Abba, you know all things and you know we have a tendency to waver between two opinions. That in our belief, doubt is right there beside us holding us down and keeping us back. And at times we let this doubt overtake us and cause us to stumble. Please forgive us. Please help us not to just believe, but to have faith. The faith that comes from your Son. Please show us our weaknesses so that in them, we may be strong through Messiah.

Abba, I pray for the Church. I pray that they would become your Ekklésia. Not buildings made by the hands of men, but a body that is built by Yeshua himself. The Church is looking for you; they are seeking Yeshua. But Father, in your eyes, do they look like your Son? When you see them, do you see Yeshua or do you see the world? Are they chasing after the same things the world chases after? Are they pursuing material possessions and temporary things that will burn up in the flames; things that won't last for eternity? If they are, Abba, have mercy on them. Let them become your Ekklésia and let your Ekklésia be a light in a dark place.

As the body of Messiah, we are supposed to be salt and light. Are we salt? Are we light? Abba, wake us up! Don't let the world look upon your Ekklésia as weak and broken and defeated and looking just like them. When they look upon us, let them see you. Let them see unshakeable faith.

And when the whole world crumbles around us, we do not move. This is His faith. Help us to find it. Help us to be faith on the earth.

Father Almighty, the world is making a mockery of you. And I know you are a merciful and loving Elohim and that you are patient, but Abba, please, show your face. Show this world that you are the One who created it. And that by your power it continues and that by your power it will cease. Show this world what it means to fear you.

For there are so many people going about doing worldly things thinking that they can find happiness and joy and peace in those things; in stuff. And they may find brief moments of happiness, but it never lasts. The joy and the peace that comes from you lasts forever. Abba, have mercy. Help us to know you as you really are. Not how we have created you to be, but as you really are. Oh Abba, show us your glory.

Yeshua said he went to prepare a place for us. And that in the Father's house are many rooms and if it were not true, He would have told us. Let us hear the words of your Son. Let us hear His call. Let us hear the words, "Well done thy good and faithful servant, come and share in your Master's happiness."

We know time is short, and whether Yeshua comes, or our lives, which are but a vapor, come to an end, one of these days we will stand before you. And I ask in the name of Yeshua, that we would hear those words, "Well done." And whatever time we have left before His return or before we go, for you know our days, help us to bring glory to your name.

For you are not wanting anyone to perish, but that all would come to repentance, even the most wretched and the most wicked among us. You want them to come to repentance too. Use us to find those that are lost. Use us to snatch some from the fire and save them. Use us to take your name to the ends of the earth. Use us, not because we are special, but because you are worthy!

In the name of Yeshua I pray. Amen.

Dear Reader,

Congratulations! You made it! Thank you for taking the time to read this book. I hope you learned something new about the Father and His Son. And I hope it has given you even more enthusiasm to be a witness for Yeshua on the earth. Even more enthusiasm to show this world... **Faith That Is His**. Now, *Go, stand and speak in the temple to the people all the words of this life. (Acts 5:20)*

Taw: (THE END)
Looking unto Yeshua the author and finisher of our faith... (Hebrews 12:2)

Resources

את

Strong's Exhaustive Concordance
Brown-Driver-Briggs Hebrew Lexicon
Thayer's Greek Lexicon
The Berean Interlinear
The Interlinear Hebrew-Greek-English Bible with
Strong's Concordance
NAS Exhaustive Concordance
Ancient Hebrew Learning Center
TheLivingWord.com
BibleHub.com
BlueLetterBible.org
King James Bible

About the Author

את

Tracy heard the father's call in 2002. Several years ago, she fully embraced this calling and began following Father's instructions. She has studied the pictograph of the Ancient Hebrew Alphabet and has learned how it helps us understand the Scriptures in a more definitive and concrete sense.

She is dedicating the rest of her life to the work of the Kingdom. She is currently in the process of writing other books which she hopes will honor the Father, will serve as a witness of Yeshua, and will help strengthen and encourage the body of Messiah.

In Thy Laws...
I did not know to keep thy commandments.
I had been taught that they were done away with.
But it is in thy laws that I have found freedom.
And I will never go back to the ways of the heathen.

Made in the USA
Monee, IL
12 April 2021